HOW TO BUY A HOUSE

E. Jayashree Kurup

Collins magicbricks.com

First published in India in 2015 by Collins
An imprint of HarperCollins *Publishers*

Building 10, Tower A, 4th Floor, DLF Cyber City, Phase II,
Gurugram Haryana – 122002, India
www.harpercollins.co.in

P-ISBN: 978-93-5177-268-2
E-ISBN: 978-93-5177-269-9

2 4 6 8 10 9 7 5 3 1

Typeset in 12/15 Garamond Regular at
SÜRYA

Printed and bound at
MicroPrints India, New Delhi

CONTENTS

HOW TO BUY A HOUSE

E. Jayashree Kurup is Head, Content and Research, at Magicbricks.com.

Jayashree has been a business journalist for over two decades with *The Times of India*, *The Economic Times* and *The Financial Express*. She writes extensively on real estate and infrastructure, city management, information technology, human resources and management. She joined Magicbricks in 2006 and set up the content and research department for the brand. She has spearheaded many research initiatives such as PropIndex-India's Apartment Index, Housing Sentiment Index in association with IIM-Bangalore and the Value Analysis Report.

Jayashree is involved with a number of global research initiatives and specializes in analysing research data to provide usable solutions to users. She also works with businesses in using industry dialogues such as Real Estate Dialogues (RED) and Broker's Connect with senior management in her domains of expertise to generate content solutions that keep audience and industry engaged. She forayed into research in 2002 as Head, Asia Pacific Research, Real Estate, with Insignia Brooke, a global property consultancy, headquartered in New York, where she analysed the real estate markets of India, China, Thailand, Philippines and Japan.

In 2014, Jayashree won the Best Journalist Award of the Construction Industry Development Council (CIDC) Vishwakarma Awards.

She is a regular guest columnist in a number of established media including The Times Group and others. She is an Executive Member of the CII Real Estate Committee as well as a Jury member for the Construction Industry Development Council (CIDC) Vishwakarma Awards. She holds a postgraduate diploma in journalism from the Times School of Journalism and is a postgraduate in English Literature from the Miranda House, Delhi University.

Jayashree is a natural impressionist painter who enjoys walking nature trails and popular Hindi and English music from the '60s.

INTRODUCTION

I have been a real estate journalist in print and online media for over fifteen years. So I have become the de facto advisor on property matters. And that is a lot of advice, believe me! At weddings and parties, in metros and during morning walks, potential buyers keep lurking, waiting for the most appropriate moment to slip in their property question, seemingly casually, into the conversation. I had stashed away all these real-life situations and incidents in the recesses of my memory till I started writing this book. As I warmed up, the characters took a life of their own and I found that I did not have to go anywhere else to understand the everyday problems of common people.

In the last few years I have seen developers organizing themselves into an industry—the outcome is still awaited. However, parallely, I have seen consumers evolving from scared buyers who think a hundred times before taking a decision to confident investors, using property investment to plan retirement for parents and for themselves. They take multiple loans for different projects and treat real estate as an important part of their investment portfolio. From helpless property seekers consumers are evolving into militant pressure groups who are not afraid to take on defaulting developers to consumer courts and even the Competition Commission of India.

However, no matter how savvy or serious you are as a consumer, there are some basic rules of the thumb that can guide you along. Those rules are currently what drive coffee-table discussions at various parties and discussion forums. They are part of the collective conscience of urban India and are articulated in various stages of the buying process by developers, builders, brokers, agents, aunties-next-door, family friends and a host of others in your ecosystem. Whether they know enough about property or the business or not, everyone has an opinion about how you should take the crucial decision of buying a house.

In the past ten years a host of experts from across the industry, including developers, big agents, municipal heads and financial experts, have appeared on various Magicbricks.com forums telling users how best to buy the house of their dreams. Be it the first, second or even the third home, there is no substitute for personal research. This has been documented in a special section on Magicbricks.com and titled advice.Magicbricks.com. I am an ardent advocate of this practice of Buyer Serve Thyself. So read on and I hope this book helps you in your buying decision.

1

SHOULD YOU BUY A HOUSE?

WHEN SHOULD YOU BUY A HOUSE?

When my friend Lakshmi, who works at the United Nations and has travelled the world for over a decade, called to say she was buying a house in the National Capital Region of Delhi, it triggered a train of thought that culminated in this book.

'Why are you buying a house?' I had asked her.

She sounded baffled. 'To live in, of course.'

So, had she decided what to buy?

'Yes, my brother's colleague invested with a certain developer along the Noida Expressway and we figured we could do the same with a budget of Rs 1.5 crore. I was just calling to check,' she said smugly.

She had made up her mind to buy a house, and

then relied on another person's selection to decide on a suitable one. Who may have, in turn, relied on yet another person's judgement! After all, if it is right for him, why not for me?

The problem came when I asked if her lifestyle matched that of her brother's colleague. She had no idea how he lived, what he did in his spare time or whether his friends and relatives were scattered all over town like hers were. My question had stumped her.

So let's start with the basic question: Why is it necessary to own property? In a country like India, where there is no social security, a house symbolizes a shelter from all sorts of storms. Beyond the comfort and security that owning a home offers, it has many more tangible benefits as well. It forms an asset that is likely to bring in good returns on one's investment.

When you start thinking about buying a house, the most common question that springs to mind is: When is the right time to buy a house? My answer would be: The 'right' time is when *you* feel you are ready for the responsibility that goes hand-in-hand with the buying.

To make the right choice, it is important to consider your objectives of buying a house first. Why do you want a house? What motivates you to go for a particular one? Do you want to buy a house because you want to live in it, or are you looking for some extra source of income that a house can fetch in the form of rent? Or, are you simply buying it for long-term value leverage?

The clearer you are in your mind about why you should

buy a house, the more focussed your search will be and the better will you be able to select one that meets your requirements.

Admiral and Mrs Singh had spent their lives in a plush home in Vasant Vihar. Their friends were all easily accessible and they had a hectic social life. When Admiral Singh had his first niggling health problems, his daughter, who lived abroad, came over to help them out. However, when he reached a stage where he needed help with the maintenance of the house, paying taxes and visiting doctors, it seemed logical to move to a place where his daughter could coordinate with a management services firm for maintenance, where safety and security were taken care of by closed-circuit television cameras, which was situated in a less crowded part of the city and close to his medical centre. He bought a much smaller house in upscale Gurgaon in a premium facility. The house was more compact but luxurious, maintenance was the agency's headache and the hospital that treated him was comfortable servicing him as it was closer home and the streets were less crowded than the Vasant Vihar main roads. His agent helped him sell his large bungalow and purchase the more compact premium apartment.

Clearly Admiral and Mrs Singh's house-hunting approach would be very different from that of Lakshmi's. Although both are end-users seeking a secure home within a gated community, while one was looking at social infrastructure in terms of hospital and so on, the other was looking at a life that matched her cosmopolitan lifestyle.

Now take the case of Chandrika Maini, a single working woman in Delhi. She needed a house of her own. However her criteria were a small, safe, well-maintained house in a complex that was convenient, met her lifestyle needs and was in a good neighbourhood. She bought a small two-bedroom unit that was launched by a private developer in a part of Gurgaon that was not too expensive but had future potential in terms of value increase of real estate. The developer delayed the project and she is yet to get possession of her apartment, but she does not regret the decision because she feels she could not have afforded the current property rates.

Clearly, even when safety and maintenance are the common points among all the three examples that I cited, the nuances and detail of the requirement make all the difference. Understand those nuances and see that you find a house that addresses your specific requirements. This is important because small issues can become lifetime irritants.

WHAT MAKES MORE SENSE: RENTING OR BUYING?

The question of whether you should choose to stay in a house on rent or try and buy your own is one that troubles many across the world. There are tools that help you compute whether it makes financial sense to stay on rent or buy a property. Check out the Magicbricks Buy vs Sell Calculator which can serve as a broad indicator on whether you should lease or buy. However, even the best calculators cannot give you the personalized advice that can serve you best when facing such a dilemma. The trick is to logically think your problem through.

Most of us would like to own a house. However, remember that you can only buy in a locality that matches your budget. If you want the convenience of staying near your place of work, in a locality that matches your lifestyle needs and where you are close to friends or family, buying may not be the best option for you. Also, if the property rates are very high in your city, buying is often not the best option.

For starters, do a SWOT—Strength, Weakness, Opportunity, Threat—analysis. First, pin down the locality where you would like to stay and the type of house you are looking for. Now identify an outflow that you would be comfortable paying every month. If you find a house that you would like to stay in, which is close to your workplace or easily accessible from there, go for it. But the question is whether you can actually afford to buy it in your current circumstances.

Remember that the Equated Monthly Instalment (EMI) on your property should not be over 40 per cent of your monthly salary. That way you would be comfortable paying it back. After all, you need to have enough money to manage your basic necessities and also be able to save a small bit while maintaining your existing lifestyle. Furthermore, when you decide to buy, you need to have 10-15 per cent of the cost as your personal contribution to the purchase, as banks do not lend 100 per cent. Decide on buying only if these issues can be managed. Otherwise, take a house on rent and start saving towards that initial down payment.

Let me give you a rule of the thumb. Let's say you pay Rs 100 as rent every month. If you find a house that fits your requirements and the EMI would be about 25 per cent more than your rental value, i.e. Rs 25 more per month, go for it and purchase the new house. The outflow would require you to make a few lifestyle changes to be able to pay initially. But as annual salary increases, this 25 per cent extra will cease to be an irritant. Also remember that the pay-out will result in ownership.

There are other scenarios where a combination of buy plus rent works. Take, for instance, Naveen Lambah, who lived a comfortable life in Mumbai and was proud to stay in the house that he and his wife had designed early in their married life. The challenge came when Naveen was transferred to Delhi. They had two options: sell in Mumbai and buy in Delhi or lease out the house in Mumbai and take one on rent in Delhi. However, when he checked the sales values, he discovered that the property markets were not buoyant at the time and he was not getting the right value for the property. So he leased out his furnished apartment in Mumbai to a tenant who had moved in from another city. But Lambah's budget did not allow him to buy a house in Delhi and he has stayed in Delhi on rent for over seven years now. His search for a house has only recently borne fruit and he is purchasing a property in a locality of his choice. The current slow market conditions allowed him to secure a good bargain and buy a ready-to-move-in unit. He feels he is a winner because the high rental values in Mumbai not only helped him pay the rent in Delhi but also helped him save some amount towards the home buying kitty over the past seven years.

HOW TO CHOOSE A PLACE TO RENT

When you buy a property, your choice of locality is limited to areas where properties are available within your budget. But when you are looking at renting a property, your canvas is much wider. So it is always good to make a checklist.

Budget is a prime consideration. Check your finances and see how much you can allocate to rent. This should be an amount that you will be able to pay month-on-month. Accommodate it within your house rent allowance package, or just a tad over, for best results.

Now assess how big your accommodation should be. Remember that you have not only to take up lodging, but also service it monthly, including the maintenance and municipal charges which have to be paid by the tenant. Paying the annual property taxes and asset maintenance are the responsibility of the landlord.

Ensure that facilities such as public transport, security and daily grocery needs are easily accessible. These make your stay more comfortable. Transport connectivity with minimum traffic pressure points makes the daily commute to work less stressful. Look for a neighbourhood where you have like-minded people staying in the vicinity so that there is minimum clash of interests.

HOW TO CHOOSE A PLACE TO BUY

There are many residential formats to choose from:

- Residential plots
- Apartments
- Single floors
- Independent houses
- Multi-storey flats

The table on page 11 is an illustration of how each type of property is represented city-wise on the Magicbricks.com portal. This is a representation of property profiles listed for sale across some large and small cities.

Each type of property has its own advantages and disadvantages.

Plot Vs Multi-storey Apartments

In India, plots are much in demand. Even today, most small cities are witnessing more demand for plots than for apartments. Most cities grow organically from smaller towns and being a homeowner is equated with owning a plotted development which can accommodate the growing family needs.

The apartment culture is very much a big city trend and has been the norm only in Mumbai where the population density is high with very little land to accommodate the teeming masses. In most large cities, development authorities and private developers have traditionally sold plotted development in layouts. Consumers opted for these as it was the bulk of the supply. The other option

Cities	Single-Floor Units (%)	Multi-Storey Apartments (%)	Independent Houses (%)	Residential Plots (%)	Villas (%)
Bengaluru	11	56	6	23	4
Chennai	32	24	7	32	5
Hyderabad	5	38	11	39	7
Mumbai	2	92	4	1	1
New Delhi	57	33	6	3	1
Pune	2	88	2	5	3

**Multi-storey apartments also include penthouses and studio apartments.

was group housing in the G+3 or G+4 formats. These were not usually serviced with lifts until the twenty-first century and therefore did not carry the premium tag.

In most large cities, development of apartments along economic corridors started in the 1990s, when the first National Housing and Habitat Policy was announced and structured housing finance at affordable rates were announced to retail investors. This triggered a movement primarily in the suburbs and peripheral areas where young consumers bought apartments within gated communities. Here, common amenities and enhanced security were the drivers. The apartment came packaged with lifestyle features such as clubs, sport complexes and entertainment options.

Since the economic drivers were largely restricted to big cities, the apartment culture caught on here. In smaller cities many investors bought apartments but have not had great success in exiting them. Only those abutting economic hubs—where a floating population from other states and cities occupy the flats while working in the city—have had success. Those working in Information Technology (IT) and IT Services companies have bought or leased apartments there. They have no affiliation to the city's traditional residential hubs and prefer suburbs close to their place of work with good social infrastructure such as schools, hospitals, entertainment and shopping centres.

So How Do You Choose a Plot?

Plotted developments are sold either by development authorities or government entities responsible for aggregating land for city development. From the 1960s to the 1990s, land was aggregated by city authorities and then released as plots for houses to retail buyers. A city's municipal corporation is entrusted with the master-planning of the city and it lays down building bye-laws which determine how much construction can take place on the plotted developments. Then there is a process by which this development takes place.

The development authority is responsible for aggregating land and getting titles changed to facilitate residential/commercial/retail development. It also decides on layouts and what quantity of land is to be released in what time frame. Once the layouts are planned, they are declared publicly and opened to retail investors as structured layouts. Buyers can apply for these developments and if they get chosen in the draw of lots, they are allotted plots of land. The buyer cannot choose the plot of land he or she decides to buy and has to wait for the allotment process. The development authorities normally take 2-5 years to hand over the developed land to buyers. Once handed over, these are ready for use. Water, power and telecom lines are built, roads are developed and basic services such as transport integration is planned out. Now the plots are ready for the retail buyer to build upon. Building the house on the plots will then be an independent activity that will have to be undertaken by the owner.

The other source of securing plotted units is from private developers, within their townships or developments. Most developers sell plots at early stages of their development so they can raise money to start the development work. The developer can only sell the plots once he has received approval from the municipal corporation or the district town and country planning office to sell residential plots on that land. They may either reach out to the public through advertisements/mailers or other promotional activity, or engage the services of brokers/agents to sell on their behalf.

When buying directly from developers, buyers need to read the brochures carefully for location, services and other facilities promised. This is important as the buyer has to tally these with what will be delivered approximately two years down the line after completion of development work. Brokers/agents can help identify the best plots which the consumer may not be able to do on his own as there is nothing on the ground to base the search on. However, it is important to visit the site and check out the land on which the plots are being sold. Agents also help interact with developers and conclude the transaction until registration of the property. Good-quality agents can handhold consumers until the handover stage as well.

The consumer needs to check the track record of developers and also study the details of the project and the approvals secured. There are a few private land aggregators too who sell small plotted developments in many areas. They have no development background and may have been land aggregators who sell to consumers at rates lower than those normally available. These are risky buys.

A development authority can only sell a plotted

development in an area that has been master-planned by the city planners or the municipal authorities and the basic social infrastructure such as local retail, dispensaries, schools, etc. have been provided for. The approvals for selling the layouts are given only after the basic planning for social infrastructure have been made according to planning specifications. You as the customer are within your rights to ask for the overall township layout to ensure that these facilities have been provided for.

Initially, care and maintenance of the property is undertaken by the development authority and later handed over to the Residents' Welfare Association (RWA). Any RWA is a general corpus of all buyers into the layout which registers as a separate entity and elects an executive team that is authorized to manage the development after it is completed and handed over. The allotment of plots is generally made through a drawing of lots and the buyer has little control over the profile of the neighbourhood.

When private developers sell plotted developments, these are normally within gated communities with the management in the hands of the developer for at least an initial period of about three years. Since the developers are normally concerned about the upkeep of their developments as they add to their reputation, these are relatively premium. They are privately sold through agents or advertisements in public media. The buyer can select his or her unit based on personal specifications such as location, the direction it faces or even access to facilities.

The other option is to go for an apartment in a multi-storey complex, which is becoming the norm in urban areas where the cost of land is too high to be affordable and apartments offer easy convenience and better security. This has pushed up the demand for apartments with the demand coming primarily from the younger generation of professionals between twenty-five and forty-five years of age. Normally employed with the IT or other services sectors, they seek community living with lifestyle features such as club house, jogging track and sport and entertainment facilities within the layout.

Says a premium developer in Hyderabad, 'Youngsters coming to work in the IT areas of Hitec City and Madhapur from other cities will not stay anywhere but within a five-kilometre radius. Their only interest in the city is the IT district and the work/leisure culture it offers. Youngsters from Hyderabadi families who work here, however, do not mind buying in areas slightly distant if they are more affordable.'

Independent Plot or Apartment Within a Gated Community?

The gated community is a form of residential complex sometimes characterized by high walls and fences. There is common security and managed facilities. Many have basic grocery facilities available within the complex. There are parks, recreational and sport facilities too. It often boasts of controlled entrances, surveillance of those entering and exiting the premises, clean surroundings and amenities. These communities offer freedom from the hassles of everyday civic problems, ranging from water cuts and pebble-strewn streets to living with the stench of unpicked garbage cans. Basics of everyday living such as newspaper delivery, carwash, garbage chutes, street and common area lighting, etc. are taken care of. Even plumbing, electrical and maintenance services are available as a common service. This format is now quite usual in suburban areas of cities. In select cases as in Chennai, for instance, these communities have come up within city areas where old plotted developments have been redeveloped into modern apartment complexes.

Such apartments within gated communities by a reputed developer are normally safe bets for you the consumer. However, do take stock of social infrastructure within 5-10 km radius of your house. This includes schools, hospitals, parks, entertainment and retail facilities. As already mentioned, many gated communities provide basic grocery facilities within the complex itself.

An independent house has other advantages however. First, it is generally customized to the buyer's requirements in terms of the type of materials used for the finishing of floors, walls, bathrooms and kitchen fittings. Even the format can be tailored to lifestyle requirements such as libraries, party areas, pooja rooms, etc. It can also provide ample open space and clutter-free living. Even when plot sizes are small, users have the option to divide facilities on different floors. For instance, I know a designer who purchased a sixty-square-yard plot and created a boutique apartment with facilities spread on three floors. That way the requirements of living/dining and bedroom spaces are spread over different floors. The specifications were international quality and modular storage took care of the space crunch.

In apartments the usable area is far lower than the super area that a buyer pays for as it includes driveways, corridors, lifts and lobbies, atrium, etc. The ratio of super to carpet area is much lower at 8-15 per cent in plotted developments, unlike in multi-storey apartments where it can be as much as 40 per cent. This means the consumer has more usable space in independent units than in apartments, as there is a much smaller common area that accounts for the missing carpet area in apartments.

Whatever the choice, make sure you pre-determine who is to look after the common facilities such as roads, water, power supply and back-ups. When you buy, the responsibility rests normally with the developer or the development authority. Find out the norms in your city and if it has to pass on to the RWA, then it is important you know the profile of your neighbourhood so that like-minded members will ensure the quality of the upkeep according to your expectations. Sometimes when you buy a housing unit at a rate lower than the rest of the market, you may be sacrificing on the quality of neighbours and end up having to struggle with the quality of upkeep of your locality.

In suburban locations of cities driven by professionals such as Chennai, Bengaluru, Gurgaon and Pune, there are some developments where villas or townhouses are provided within the gated complex with all the advantages that normally come with apartments. These are more expensive but a safer and hassle-free option. However, you should be prepared to pay enhanced maintenance charges for these facilities.

Single-floor Unit Vs Multi-storey Apartment

A single-floor apartment is one where the builder buys a piece of land, often old plots which are up for redevelopment, constructs flats on each floor according to the permissible Floor Area Ratio (FAR) and building bye-laws, and sells them as independent apartments on each floor. These FARs and bye-laws vary from city to city and you need to consult your local municipal authority to determine the rates in your city. The land belongs proportionately to all the buyers of the single floors. Since there are a smaller number of units than in a multi-storey apartment complex, single-floor units lack economies of scale and so have few common facilities such as maintenance and electricity back-up as compared to larger multi-storey apartments.

But these units on redeveloped plots in prime downtown areas, where plotted development was the norm earlier, are bringing new-format apartments in premium locations. Since they normally do not go above four floors, they do not need common power back-up for lifts and common maintenance and come at a price lower than multi-storey units. Also, since there are no long corridors or common parking space as in apartments that need to be landscaped and maintained, the monthly maintenance charges are lower.

Of late they have also made a comeback in suburban locations such as Gurgaon when the Haryana government allowed single units to be sold as independent units. In Noida, however, single floors are not allowed to be sold and registered as single units. Currently, premium old plotted sectors are not witnessing redevelopment as new buyers are looking for smaller units and not large residential houses.

A multi-storey apartment is the most preferred housing unit in metros today. It is a cluster of apartments in a high-rise building developed on a plot with all amenities available within a gated community. These units can be aggregated and constructed by developers or in the cooperative mode as Cooperative Group Housing Societies (CGHS). The cooperative housing format was very popular in the 1990s when employees of various public and private sector corporations got together and registered housing societies which were then allotted houses by the development authorities in the city. These were constructed in a format that had a G+7 format at least, depending on the city's bye-laws. While basic common facilities come with the apartments such as lifts and power back-up, you need to be sure of the quality of services in the complex as there are no set benchmarks. These services are offered to residents for a fee that is levied as monthly maintenance charge. They usually cover water and power supply, including back-ups, lift and common area maintenance, and landscaping. Many developments also provide plumbing and electrical services for a fee.

WHERE SHOULD YOU BUY?

When you choose to buy a property, price is a good starting point. See what you are comfortable paying. Then check out the locations that offer you options within your budget. Of these, premium localities in downtown areas will be more expensive and you will have to settle for smaller units to fit your budget. As you move further away, you will get larger units as the per-square-foot price reduces.

There will always be a price difference between different locations that is proportionate to its strategic placement. For instance, if the unit is close to a flyover or a metro station and therefore easily accessible, it will come at a much higher price than one that is more difficult to reach. Locations near crowded traffic lights can decrease in value. Staying close to schools, hospitals, etc. can be a double-edged sword. If you are too close and have to put up with the parking problems that come with these large public facilities in the vicinity, prices go down. However, if you are close enough but are not impacted by the huge floating population visiting these facilities, you will have to pay more for it.

Having good-quality water and regular power, access to transport services and schools, hospitals, malls and entertainment complexes push up values.

It is quite possible that a particular area has good infrastructure, access to markets and places of entertainment but if it is loaded with existing and upcoming residential projects, then the price rise in that area may not be dramatic but a gradual one. For price rise is determined by the gap between demand and supply. The greater the supply over demand, the better the chance of getting a good deal. This often leads to discounting by sellers and tough bargaining by buyers. On the other hand, if there is a greater demand and limited supply, it becomes a sellers' market where sellers tend to hold values and there is little scope for negotiation as more buyers chase a smaller number of properties.

You can make an estimate of the number of available and proposed flats in an area through a good broker and ascertain the past price movement in the short term. You can also check online at property portals to assess the number of properties that are listed for sale in that area. While finalizing the location of your house, these are the things you should keep in mind:

- The location should be within the approved or sanctioned master plan of the local government/ authorities.
- It should have good connectivity and there should not be significant chronic problems such as traffic bottlenecks within the micro-location or water logging during the rains.
- Infrastructure such as power, water supply, drainage and sewerage should be in place.

- Location should be within easy reach of an active business hub and educational institutions, hospitals, IT parks, entertainment hubs, etc. Access is the operative term here. Even if the location is a little farther away but has good access by road or train to the business hub, it has value.

WHICH IS THE BEST TIME FOR BUYING?

There have been numerous cases of delay in delivery by developers for various reasons over the past few years. There are international citizens who have filed FIRs at police stations in Gurgaon because the premium house they have booked has not been handed over to them even after ten years after signing of papers. A group of high-profile buyers took a prominent developer to the Competition Commission of India for alleged violations and won the case too. In many instances, it is a delay in approvals from the city authorities that delays the projects.

In such a scenario, if you have the required finances, ready-to-move-in is the ideal option for you as an end-user. This property would be significantly more expensive than at the launch stage but you as a buyer are protected against time and cost over-runs. Since the project structure is ready and possession will take place shortly, you are assured of the time frame within which you will be able to occupy the house. It also saves you from paying the EMI during the period when the house is under construction. If you are buying a house for future use or even to serve as a means to supplement your income through regular rental returns, ready-to-move-in property brings immediate rental income which also helps repay the loan secured to buy the property.

Of late, developers across cities have been offering interesting subvention schemes where you can pay a small token amount at the time of booking and maybe another instalment later. The bulk of the money is paid only after the construction is complete and the house is ready for possession. This way, you as the consumer feel more protected as your investment is much lower in the beginning and the bulk of the payment is made as the construction progresses or when the apartment is ready. From the 30:70 or 20:80 ratios that developers offered a few years ago, the scene has dramatically changed. Now you can enter the home-buying cycle by paying a mere 10 per cent of the cost of the house. The developer is given the loan by the bank on your behalf and he even services the EMIs until possession. You have to start paying only once the house is completed.

These schemes normally come into play when markets remain weak for a period of time and do not show any real tendency to revive. Developers then use such schemes to revive interest and make the consumer commit to a purchase.

You may ask: why would a developer pay on your behalf? Developing a house is a long-term activity and is capital-intensive. However, during the economic slowdown in India when inflation was very high, interest rates went up significantly and banks also declared real estate a high-risk sector and reduced lending. Developers needed to keep constructing and commercial loans came at very high rates of interest. In such a scenario, the industry came up with a scheme where the bank issued a retail loan to an individual like you but the developer took on the responsibility of paying the interest at retail rates. This way you needed to pay a small amount at the beginning thus showing your interest. But you were protected from delays by not having to pay until possession. The developer received the loan from the bank at lower rates of interest.

If you are a new investor with limited finances, look for an under-construction property with a suitable payment plan and keep a horizon of 2-3 years for possession. But make sure you go for a reputed builder. When you purchase a house at the pre-launch or launch stage, the buyer pays in smaller instalments linked to the progress of construction but he also has a longer waiting period before the asset is liveable or starts paying for itself.

This option is good in new and evolving growth areas on the peripheries of cities where infrastructure itself is under development and there is a waiting period before it becomes liveable. Since both infrastructure and housing are being developed simultaneously, the user gets the advantage of moving in when both are ready. It also comes cheaper as property values are always lower when the infrastructure in the area is under development. The downside of this type of property is that possession will happen only after a minimum of 24-36 months. During this period the end-user will have to shell out both the monthly rental for the place they stay in and the EMI for the new property.

HOW SHOULD YOU GO ABOUT IT?

Globally consumers consider second- or third-sale houses as they come cheaper than newer ones. The Indian property market being still in the nascent stage, planned redevelopment of cities do not take place and therefore older properties, instead of being cheaper, are often more expensive as the values relate to their location in downtown or city areas while newer properties are constructed on the peripheries.

The rise of property portals has brought older properties into the formal markets through structured listings. You can search, compare or even speak to sellers and discuss and negotiate rates. Consider a few issues when you look at 'secondary markets' (that is, sales through a channel, like portals/agents; primary is when you buy direct from a seller).

First, get some legal help to ensure that titles of the property are clear and unencumbered. Investing a small amount to get this checked is worth the effort. Good brokers normally help in this process until registration of the purchased property.

Second, try and take a small loan to purchase the house as the bank will also do the due-diligence and this is a level of checking. These houses are old and require periodic maintenance. When you buy them, ensure you do an overhaul of electrical and plumbing infrastructure so that you can have a hassle-free stay.

Finally, ensure that you conclude all documentation—registration, mutation and transfers—in municipal and utilities' records to avoid any problems in the future.

DEVELOPER CHECK

Once you decide upon the locality, the next step is to check the developers who are building there.

The choice of builder is an important decision. Examine the builder's track record, his financial strength, his ability to deliver on time, construction quality and payment terms, especially in the case of a local builder. Do a background check on developers and assess where you would feel safe to make your investment. You should also check with local real-estate brokers the last transaction price or the price of similar property in that location.

The best way to do this is to do your own research. Find out who the developers are and what they have to offer. This applies only to new property. They normally advertise through newspapers, portals, etc. Another good check is to log on to the new projects sections of property portals and go through the locality-wise information where you can get the profiles of projects and the developers. Tally the names of selected developers with associations such as the Confederation of Real Estate Developers Association of India (CREDAI) and National Real Estate Developers Council (NAREDCO). Most developers are members of these associations and their profiles are posted there. Most also maintain their own websites. Make sure you scrutinize as many of these as possible as there is no official site where you can check out the antecedents of developers.

Once you have shortlisted the property, examine the floor plans and the types of property each developer is constructing. Much of this information is available online so this can be done at your convenience. Once you have shortlisted some properties, do your own footwork. Check out the projects on-site. Get an expert broker to show you around. When choosing the broker, too, follow the same process of checking online for their profile, and try to work with someone who has serviced somebody you know well. Personal recommendations are best while choosing brokers. There are also broker networks such as the National Association of Realtors and ReMax. Identify brokers and agents who are associates in these associations.

Ultimately, you have to do your own scouting. Sometimes what looks good on paper may not feel right when you see it on the ground. The documents may say that the size of the unit is a certain number of square feet. However, when you actually see the sample apartment or the layout on the ground, it may not match your expectation. There is no alternative to physical verification especially in India. If you are not able to do so, try getting family or friends to make a tour on your behalf.

About ten years ago my husband and I decided we

wanted to buy a house to live in. Working in the sector, I knew what to look for and how to go about it. However, we saw a dozen houses that met all our specifications on paper but we could not connect with any when we visited the sites. Finally, we stumbled upon a house that as soon as we walked into our eyes lit up.

Buying a house is not simply a monetary decision. It is important to connect with the house for you to be happy there. Sometimes just a window in the wrong place can make you uncomfortable.

After considering all the above, what is most essential is your ability to negotiate! This means leveraging the available information and a fair understanding of the points discussed to strike a good deal.

Remember that the 'area' concept is used varyingly in the housing industry. Some builders and sellers take advantage of this ambiguity. A few facts to remember:

- Carpet area is defined as the precise area within the walls of your home. If you had to lay out a wall-to-wall carpet in your entire home, the area covered would be the carpet area.
- Built-up area is inclusive of not just the carpet area but also the area occupied by the walls of your house.
- Super built-up area takes into account all the area under the common spaces, which is the apartment's proportionate share of the lobby, staircase, elevator and the corridor outside the apartment.

The confusion over the super built-up area arises over what is exactly included in it and the fact that it often varies from builder to builder. Some may even include the terrace, the security room, the electrical room and/or the pump room. So find out what your builder exactly means when he uses the term. The cumulative total of these 'extras' is taken into account and divided by the number of apartments in proportion to their size. So keep in mind:

- If you get a quote for 1000 square feet, find out immediately if it is the carpet area or the super built-up area.
- There is no fixed ratio of super built-up to built-up or carpet area. Generally, the ratios in multi-storey apartments are about 35-40 per cent loading. This means that you get to use only 60-65 per cent of the area you paid for.
- In a single-floor unit on plotted developments, there is very little loading of common areas, mostly to the tune of 10-15 per cent. As a result, you get carpet areas of 85-90 per cent of the space you paid for.

Here are some tips to guide you in buying the property of your dreams:

- Check for proper conveyance of title in favour of the builder, i.e., the property title should be in the developer's name.
- Check the licence/development right/approvals from municipal and town and country planning departments in the city.

- Check clear and marketable title of the project—does the developer have the right to develop and sell the project?
- Ensure execution of proper Allotment Letter/Sale Agreements on your payments.
- Ensure whether reputed financial companies approve the project—this will help you in getting financial loans. Normally developers tie up with financial institutions to lend to the retail buyers. If your bank is not registered, you may have to secure all the papers from the developer and get the processing done individually for your loan.
- See the tentative layout/building plan provided by the builder.
- Ask for occupation/completion certificate if you are purchasing a completed project where possession has been handed over.
- Finally, ensure the Conveyance Deed is registered after the entire payment has been made. This ensures that the property titles are in your name. If there is a loan from a financial institution, this property will be hypothecated to the bank until the loan is repaid.

Deciding to purchase, determining your choice and then sorting out the fine print and getting into the nitty gritty of buying a house may seem daunting at first. However, approach the exercise scientifically and make sure you are driven by facts and information. After all, it is your money, your property and your lifestyle that is at stake. The best way to ensure that you have made the right choice is to do your own research. Use the data that is available online and in print and then go and check the sites on your own. Take charge and move forward. You will find that being armed with the right information can make the whole exercise enjoyable and fulfilling.

2

SHORTLISTING YOUR PROPERTY

THE MANY FACTORS

Govind Bhan is a mid-level executive with a multinational. His wife works, and they have two children under the age of ten. Moving from Bengaluru to Delhi was a big decision for him. His one consideration was that he should be close to his place of work to reduce the daily commute. Since he worked in Noida, an eastern suburb of Delhi, he decided to look for a house there. As he has school-going children, he needed to be near international schools. He was also looking for retail and entertainment options as the family was used to such a lifestyle in Bengaluru. The announcement of the launch of the night safari, the NH-7

Weekender music carnival in Greater Noida, and the amusement parks near Noida Sector 18, worked in his favour. He found gated communities more secure. Therefore, he chose an apartment along the Noida Expressway, constructed by a well-known developer, and negotiated the price to a rate he was comfortable with. He is currently extremely satisfied with his purchase.

If you are an end-user, the size of your family, along with the budget, can be the determining factors while choosing the type of house you need. Start with your chosen budget and visit a property website such as Magicbricks.com. Post your specifications in the search box and you will get a range of property options that match your requirements. Choose the size, the number of bedrooms required, the amenities you are looking for and see which localities fit your requirements. Start narrowing down your options to the property that is the best match. Now start calling the agents or landlords who have posted the property. Visit the property if you can as that gives you the best feel of what it would be like to stay there. If the place is ready for possession, talk with the people residing in the neighbourhood. They will be able to give you the real picture on what it is like to stay in that area.

Try and drive from that location to your place of work, to your child's school, retail centres and other places you are likely to visit often. This will help you gauge how convenient the location is. If you are buying from the secondary market, visit and assess the kind of people living there. The neighbourhood is very important as those are the people you will be interacting with the most when you stay there. The quality of services available in the neighbourhood also depends on the type of neighbours you have. Whatever is in demand is what will be available.

There is a wide range to choose from today as the market abounds in various housing formats—from 1, 2, 3 and 4BHK (Bedroom-Hall-Kitchen) apartments to studios, villas and row houses to builder floors and independent houses. Multi-storey projects and townships with all amenities in one project—clubhouse, swimming pool, meditation centre, health club, departmental store, school, cinema, sports facilities and banquet/party halls—are what most end-users are looking at today. However, only a site visit can establish if the developer has given you more bedrooms but of smaller size. Sometimes you may want a more open layout and may be willing to sacrifice a bedroom for bigger sizes in the remaining units.

But why am I advising you to buy re-sale property if you are an end-user?

In the past few years, property-buying by end users has become a difficult business because projects have been delayed and buyers have had to bear the burden of paying both monthly EMIs and rent for the property they have been living in. Therefore, in the past few years, especially since 2011, a large ratio of buyers have switched to entering the property buying cycle only in the last six to eight months before possession. This is the time when property values start going up and investors sell to end-users for a higher price and exit the property. The advantage of having more end-users than investors in the development cycle is that end-users demand facilities that impact the quality of living. Occupancy also goes up if end-users are in larger numbers and you are assured of a better quality of living.

Let me give you some important tips before buying re-sale property:

Location

Property buying, you would have heard from a lot of experts, depends on location. Generally, different locations dictate different price points. There are a host of factors on which property prices depend. These are social infrastructure such as schools, hospitals, colleges, retail and entertainment hubs and, most importantly, commercial hubs with office complexes where you will most likely go to work. A classic example is Mayur Vihar Phase I in East Delhi and another is Vasant Kunj in South Delhi—both were considered far-away places with little access to infrastructure when they were created by the Delhi Development Authority (DDA). To woo buyers these units were made bigger and the prices kept nominal. However, when Noida started developing with robust social infrastructure, prices in Mayur Vihar Phase I jumped significantly. Similarly, Vasant Kunj prices rose as soon as occupancy by well-heeled gentry started. The proximity to premium South Delhi areas such as Vasant Vihar helped position it as an aspirational locality. The quality of the gentry and the facilities that were made available in Vasant Kunj determined the premium tag. Eateries, entertainment options, premium shopping centres mushroomed and property values rose and have remained high till date.

The chart below illustrates the typical growth curve that property markets follow in India. This is true across cities. Check this out against the property cycles in any city small or big, or even at the locality level as I have described before. The cycle is followed in all instances. There may be a variation in how much time each stage of the cycle takes and that is determined by extraneous factors such as availability of transport, infrastructure, commercial hubs, etc.

The Development Cycle in India

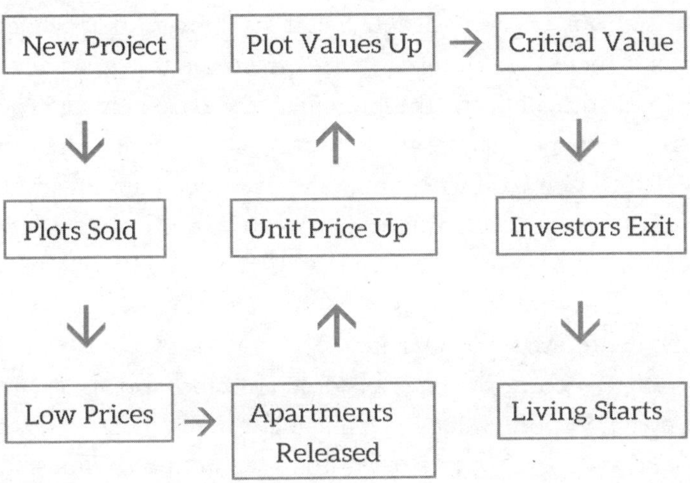

*Critical Value is when the sale price rises sufficiently to yield profit.

So do all properties close to transport infrastructure or commercial hubs do well? Not necessarily. When determining if the price of the property that you are considering will go up eventually, there are some basic issues you have to consider.

Connectivity

How well is the locality linked to highways, flyovers, metro corridors or even to main and sector roads? Sometimes if you are close to a metro corridor but are separated from the station by a crowded U-turn, you may lose out on value. Take the case of the commercial centre in downtown Bangkok in 2002 that would just not get occupied while many others in the vicinity were being leased out easily. A detailed analysis showed that while it was a mere two hundred metres from the expressway, the slip road leading to the building was extremely crowded and users did not favour that long halt. A similar situation exists in Gurgaon where the new city is separated from the old by the expressway and prices on both sides of the expressway are significantly different. Even living conditions and lifestyles are determined by which side of the expressway you stay in.

Metro corridors have become an important factor that impact property values. For instance, Magicbricks' research over the years has shown that when metro lines are announced, there is a period of euphoria when capital values of properties go up. Once construction starts and there is the resultant traffic restrictions, rental values drop by at least 25 per cent. About six months before completion, rental interest again rises and occupancy and property values start increasing. Units within 50-100 metres of metro stations post the maximum rise in values. Those places that are conveniently connected to the metros also note a rise in values. However, if the unit abuts the metro station, prices may fall because of the overcrowding and traffic jams caused by weak traffic management near stations.

In many developed economies, city managements plan for increased Floor Area Ratio (FAR) along metro corridors to accommodate the enhanced demand. In India, enhanced demand has been planned for in the new line to be created in Noida/Greater Noida. The authorities have decided to increase the FAR from the existing 2.75 to 3.5 along both sides of the proposed metro link. In Bengaluru, the FAR has been increased from 3.2 to 4 in the three years since the metro has been operational.

Another way of enhancing property values along the metro line is for large developments to work with metro authorities to create exits into the development, either townships as in Ponggol in Singapore or into commercial buildings in the vicinity as in the Suntek City in Singapore.

Social Infrastructure

Markets, schools, educational and entertainment centres as well as hospitals determine the price of residential property as well. For instance, a recent Magicbricks study on consumer preferences showed that professionals drive new residential markets near commercial hubs dedicated to information technology, finance and manufacturing. This has yielded a lifestyle that is international, cosmopolitan and youthful. As a result, the facilities that come up in these areas include international schools, entertainment hubs with all-day and much-of-the-night entertainment options and eateries that service the young workforce through all hours of the day and night. The goods stocked in the hypermarkets and lifestyle stores here are also in sync with the new demand.

How does this impact your property options? These commercial business districts are evolving into lifestyle hubs where there is the option to work hard and party harder. This includes different formats of houses such as compact high-value studio apartments, 2BHK units for young professionals as also larger format housing in 3BHK or more for the senior management. Since all facilities are concentrated near the place of work, there is less need to travel very far from home, thus reducing the stress of urban living.

A critical factor you have to consider when buying a house is the time taken to travel to your place of work, essential areas such as schools, hospitals, retail and entertainment hubs as well as to other parts of the city where your friends may live. Remember, travelling from a commercial hub to the other parts of the city is easier than travelling from the city to the commercial hub. This is because while travelling away from the commercial hub during peak hours you are likely to be against the traffic flow. However, you may also find it difficult to exit the city in the evenings as there will be peak traffic flow and you may have to alter your travel timings accordingly.

Property View

I recently decided to buy a house that would serve as a writer's retreat for me and my husband after retirement. I was looking at a corner location overlooking hills on one side and a central garden on the other. Now both these preferences came with a price tag. There is always a price differential even between different properties within the same complex or even the same building depending on the floor, the view, the size and other factors. In South India, vastu-compliant units have a premium on them. Similarly, east or south-facing properties fetch better values than north and west-facing properties, especially in north India, where winters are very cold and summers very hot. If your house faces east or south, you are likely to get more sunshine during the winter.

Users in urban areas pay more for a view. In Mumbai, for instance, the price per unit rises as you go to a higher floor. This is true of any water-facing city where the view of the water is considered a premium. The higher you go, the better the sea view. If the property is sea-facing, there is a hefty extra sum that the buyer has to shell out. Elsewhere, in high-rise apartments, the units facing the central courtyard are priced higher than those that face another apartment. Pool or park-facing properties also have a higher value. Sometimes road-facing properties are charged a premium.

In cities that are not quite used to high-rises yet, the premium is for the ground to sixth floor. Here, the consumer still clings to old-city values of living in low-rises while simultaneously availing of the safety, security and convenience that high-rises offer. As a result, they look for lower floors in high-rise condominiums. Higher floors do not command a premium vis-a-vis lower floors in such cases.

The concept of Preferred Location Charges (PLC) for new properties is based on these principles. Whatever is most in demand is considered premium and charged a PLC. For instance, if 70 per cent of buyers first ask for a corner unit, clearly at least a small percentage would be willing to pay extra to buy that unit. It is similar to what airlines do with seat pricing. Since most fliers ask for the front row, low-cost airlines charge a premium for those seats. Currently, PLC is arbitrary and there are no fixed norms for it. There are some developers who charge a PLC on every unit in a complex—this defies logic and a potential buyer needs to be aware of the extra money he is shelling out.

Area-wise Demand and Supply

Qualities such as good infrastructure, access to markets, office and entertainment hubs are common to a locality. However, the volume of units available for sale in a certain area also determines the prevailing price of a house. If it is a new growth corridor, the first project to get off the ground normally comes at a reasonable price. As more developers launch projects, it becomes an area in demand and the values keep rising steadily, normally by about 8-10 per cent every year. A developer may break the norm in an existing locality by launching a project that is richer in features and thereby commanding a higher value. Once there are a couple of projects in a locality that command a higher value, they push the base value up.

Developers too allow investors to make money by periodically revising values of projects that are still under construction. Once the new value is released, brokers and underwriters, small and big investors offload their properties at a value higher than the original sale price but lower than the new sale price. They thus book short-term profits. This happens at least 2-3 times during the development cycle. End users enter towards the end of the cycle and purchase at values that are at least 50 per cent higher than the original sale price. However, with very little holding time, they get to buy very close to possession. If you are buying on a corridor where there are several projects, examine the price and specifications of multiple projects to get the best deal. If there is more supply than demand, you stand a good chance at negotiating a better value in the secondary market.

If you are buying into a new area as an investor, remember you will get best results only if you enter early in the cycle. If you enter too late, then the first mover advantage is lost and you may not be able to exit the market for a long time as there would be a lot of ready stock and prices may remain stable. This is the case with Noida in Delhi NCR. It is a good place for end-users to buy in 2015 as there is a vast quantity of new stock ready for occupancy. But at this stage an investor should not enter the market as he will enter at a higher price but not be able to easily exit the investment at a price significantly higher than that paid.

Builder/Developer Track Record

I often get asked by users on Open House, the Magicbricks.com Discussion Forum, whether they should buy from small local developers rather than large, well-known national or regional developers as their offering fits the buyer's budget. Actually selecting a developer to buy from is a tricky business. But it can be made easier if you as a buyer are alert and do your research well.

First, whether it is a national or local developer, check the projects he has developed in the past. Physical verification of past projects is a must. If there are wet patches or peeling plaster or even badly maintained complexes, do not waste your money with this developer. If, on the other hand, you are satisfied with the quality of the structure and its maintenance, look further. Ask previous buyers what their experience has been. If the developer promised more and delivered less, you have to be on your guard. Previous buyers can also tell you whether the developer ensures good maintenance of his properties including landscaping, engineering and facility management services. This ensures good upkeep of the properties within the complex. Also check whether the developer has been delivering projects on time. In case of delays do try and find out how long the delay has been and why it happened. In some business cycles, markets have slowed down as a whole. Those can be condoned but developers who routinely delay projects cannot be your developer of choice. It is better to buy a smaller apartment from a reliable developer than go with one who promises you very large units but delays projects beyond the market benchmarks.

Check the builder's track record, his financial strength, his ability to deliver on time, construction quality and payment terms, especially in the case of a local builder. Always remember to read the fine print. Get expert assistance (lawyers, tax experts, investment consultants, valuers, banks) to do so if you will but it is important to consider de-risking your purchase as you will be spending a lot of money to buy the asset.

Funded Project

There are a number of real-estate mutual funds operating in the market currently. They lend project-wise to developers who have their account books in order and whose financials are clean. The advantage of funded projects to consumers is that the developer will not stall the project for lack of funds. The consumer can also rest a little easy as the lender does the due diligence as far as project approvals and adherence to timelines are concerned. As the project progresses and more funds are raised from consumers, the developer returns the lender's money and the project is concluded. These funds normally help the developer to bridge the working capital gap that is normally the cause for project delays.

This might seem like a lot to look for while shortlisting your property for purchase. But, in reality, it is application of common-sense combined with some simple practical tips. I have tried to summarize them into a checklist that you can carry with you and keep ticking off when looking for a property.

WHAT ARE THE DOCUMENTS YOU NEED TO CHECK BEFORE BUYING?

- Check for proper conveyance of title in favour of the developer. This ensures that the developer owns the land upon which he has built the property he is selling to you.
- Check the licence/development right/approvals of the builder. These are documents that you can ask for and the developer is mandated to show them to you.
- Ensure execution of proper Allotment Letter/Sale Agreements on your payments. An allotment letter is proof that the unit you selected and paid for is being allotted to you. Sale Agreement is a legal document that ensures that the developer has agreed to sell the property to you.
- Ensure whether reputed financial companies approve the project. This will help you in getting financial

loans. Normally developers apply to banks/financial institutions to fund retail buyers in their project. These are usually advertised. In case you are going to a bank other than those that have pre-approved the loan, you have to secure documents from the developer for them to sanction the loan. Lenders always have valuers on their payrolls to assess the potential value of the property so the lent money is safe. This helps you make a choice.

- Check the tentative layout plan and verify the plinth area. It is advisable to check the carpet area of the apartment and find if the difference between plinth area and carpet area is reasonable.
- Ask for Occupation/Completion Certificate before paying the final instalment. This is issued by the municipal authorities to the developer on completion of project.
- Ensure the Conveyance Deed is registered after the entire payment has been made. This signifies the property now legally belongs to you. This can be done only after the completion of the development and once the Completion Certificate is issued to the developer.
- For buying a property you need to check the Deed of Conveyance, Mutation Certificate (for the entire property), Land Registration Status, Sanctioned Plan, Search Report and Payment Schedule (for under-construction property). It is a must that you go through all the documents relating to the origin of

the property, chain of title, Occupancy Certificate, sanctions from various authorities dealing with building plans, fire safety and Completion Certificate.

- For re-sale property, check demand notice relating to renovation, tax dues and latest receipts of payments made towards various out-goings such as water, electricity and ground rent.

WHICH IS THE BEST STAGE TO BUY?

If you have the required finances, ready-to-move-in is the ideal option for a home buyer. For an investor, a ready-to-move-in property is feasible for business as he can buy and put it up for lease without any waiting period.

On the other hand, an under-construction property eases the financial burden wherein you can finance your property through bank loans and pay less cash up front. The downside of this type of property is that possession will happen only after a certain time period.

If you are a new investor with limited finances, look for an under-construction property with a suitable payment plan and keep a horizon of 2-3 years for possession. But make sure you go for a reputed and reliable builder.

WHICH ONE IS GOOD FOR INVESTMENT: PLOT OR FLAT?

If you choose to be a long-term investor, say 5-10 years, a plot is the best option. If you want annual returns to manage a part of your EMIs, flats are better. However, if you are investing in plots, be sure to invest in well-managed gated communities as plots are easy to encroach upon and difficult to protect. When you purchase plots within a development from a builder, the maintenance and safety of your unit is usually in the developer's hands. If you purchase from a development authority, the value of the plot is much lower but there are many instances of consumers being cheated.

Take the case of Vipin Gupta who was lucky to win a draw held by the Haryana Urban Development Authority (HUDA) in Faridabad. He duly paid his instalments and was very sure that his plot would be safe. He did not visit the plot for years until his wife and he decided to build on the plot five years after purchase. Imagine his shock when he found not only a house on it but even occupants living there for over a year. The new buyer had bought from a broker who had colluded with some HUDA officials to get documents processed in another buyer's name. This had happened not once but three times. Vipin had to pull strings to get an encumbrance-free plot assigned to him.

So after you have purchased a property, be sure to register it as soon as possible. This is mandatory so plan for these finances when you allocate your resources towards buying a house. The amount of money you need to register your property depends on its location. Cities classify localities into A, B, C and D categories and stamp duty payable while registration depends on its locality and the type of property you are purchasing. These vary from city to city and you can get the details on the municipal corporation website or from the development authority. Most buyers find it easier to use the services of an agent to get the registration done. However, you can get the registration done on your own too if you know how to deal with government departments.

Some Key Documents Required for Registering a Flat

- Chain of original conveyance.
- Sale deeds/agreement from the seller.
- Share certificate issued by the society in favour of the seller indicating membership to the society.
- NOC from the society to transfer the share in favour of the purchaser.
- Identity proof and address proof.

3

SPOT ON!

LOCATION! LOCATION! LOCATION!

The Locality

Ananya Kshirsagar was shifting to Chennai to work in a technology firm. Moving into an entirely new city where she had no friends or relatives or affiliations to any particular area, she decided to put her search for a house on hold until she actually reached the city. She worked along the Old Mahabalipuram Road (OMR), an area known for its IT offices and premium residential layouts. She decided to stay at the company's guest house and experience the city first hand to get an idea of the sectors and neighbourhoods and figure out what she should be looking for.

As soon as she arrived in Chennai, she found that since

the OMR was crowded with traffic during peak hours, it would be wise to stay close to the office to ensure she did not spend too much time commuting. She then decided to map her lifestyle. She was a compulsive shopaholic and knew she would enjoy frequent visits to shopping malls. She also looked for malls with movie theatres as she was addicted to Bollywood movies. This helped her settle on the location.

For my friend Venky, who had come to Bengaluru from overseas and did not have any attachment to any particular part of the city, the location of good international schools was the deciding factor. He chose to stay on Sarjapur Road for proximity to schools so his children did not have to travel much. He travels all the way across the city to Bannerghatta Road. 'It is better that I travel rather than my children,' he tells me.

When it comes to choosing a location, you as the consumer should look primarily at connectivity, availability of basic transport and social infrastructure in that area. Ease of living comes with ease of commute. As a result, a good starting point when deciding the location of your property is its distance from your workplace. Keep in mind the various scenarios that you will have to encounter. Are you okay with a slightly longer commute provided the neighbourhood matches your lifestyle requirements? Or, do you feel that you must go to a place close to transport corridors so that you do not have to spend too much time travelling by metro or suburban trains to your work place? Even here there are micro-nuances to consider. For instance, if you are a single woman in a city, even a lonely stretch near the metro station can be enough to disturb your safety and put your social life in jeopardy. Media person Divyashri learnt this the hard way. She stays a mere 500m from the metro station that connects directly to her office. However, because the stretch is poorly lit and lonely, she ends up driving to work and she also does not go out in the evenings for fear of the last mile.

When investing in a big city, remember a few ground rules: if you are purchasing for self-use, buy in a neighbourhood that has all the conveniences you require and also has good accessibility to the rest of the city.

The Property

We often give up the search even before it starts when we see properties that are way above our budget. It helps to keep in mind that all properties in a locality do not cost the same. There is likely to be something within a slightly wider radius that would fit your budget. Even in premium localities, if you keep searching, you will find properties that suit your budget. If you cannot afford the premium rates of the locality that you like, look for one on the fringes of your area of choice. However, remember the fringes of the locality come cheaper, because the gentry here do not match that of the premium locality you thirst for. The compromise is a pretty stiff one because this determines the quality of your social interaction within the neighbourhood. The people staying in the area may be of a different socio-economic background and you may not find them suitable neighbours.

Take the case of Vinod Nair, who was an officer in the central government. Although he had a disposable surplus, he did not have enough to buy in the premium Safdarjang Enclave which was his area of choice in South Delhi. He opted for the next best, an urban village adjoining the locality. Being less premium he could afford to buy a larger unit that accommodated the needs of his two children and his mother. Also, it had all the advantages of proximity to the main locality. The shopping and entertainment options were the same as Safdarjang Enclave. He also made a smart decision to rope in two more of his friends to buy into the same development. Now they all have each other's families to make friends with and can rely on each other's company. This may not always be possible. So make sure you check the profile of the neighbourhood. Many people have come to grief because they bought the best possible property but did not factor in noisy or otherwise unsuitable neighbours.

Age of the House

The age of the house that you select is a very critical issue. Savita Parth had been staying in middle-class Janakpuri in West Delhi since her childhood. When she looked to buy a house of her own after marriage, she opted for what she was familiar with. On the other hand, her sister Sarada was very clear that the ageing locality they lived in was now old-fashioned and so she opted for a new cooperative group housing in newly developed Dwarka, a mere 5km away. In India the older the property, the more critically you should look at it. Check out the quality of maintenance of the building. Where developers or estate managers have done a good job in the past, the property weathers better. Look at both the appearance and the functioning of the property. Plumbing, electrical and engineering issues can be major problems after you have invested in it. If not addressed and fixed once and for all, they can be a big drain on your resources as the years go by. Also, look for property that is being re-developed in city areas. They will be new and come with a maintenance-free period. Older houses come cheaper, but make sure you invest in refitting and refurbishing the old plumbing and electrical lines before moving in if you want a hassle-free stay.

A friend of mine asked me why I object to old houses because, in India, we consider buying a house a lifetime's investment. Look at it this way—did your dad sell the ancient Ambassador to buy a new one? Chances are that he did not and even if he did, it was a very emotional issue. However, today we change cars every three to five years as it saves on maintenance costs and offers a hassle-free drive.

Now look at your house. When it was bought, it matched your requirements. As families grow or shrink, the house becomes unsuitable for present needs. Also lifestyles change so rapidly that old houses seem to get dated very quickly. The living room may seem a tad too big and the bedroom a little too small. With a host of new appliances coming in, you may want a different layout for your kitchen. As lifestyles change every few years, ideally the house should go in for an overhaul every ten years. Change taps, showers, door-knobs, etc., which tend to get worn out. Not all the fixtures may be obsolete but it is worth critically examining and ruthlessly changing them even if you loved them when you bought them. Newer apartments are built to suit these requirements while older apartments have to be retrofitted to suit the changing lifestyle.

After about fifteen years, it is wise to start looking for your second house. That way you would have a new house to move into after twenty years which is the ideal life cycle of a house or apartment these days. In cities such as Singapore, which is being constantly re-planned to remain modern, older houses are put on the block for redevelopment. This is a healthy practice and ensures that the city's assets are constantly being renewed. This not only renews assets but also brings new properties into the market as new FAR norms allow more units on the same land.

There is another reason why newer houses remain on priority lists. After about ten years, traditional pooja rooms may give way to modern gadget rooms. Children's lifestyles may be modified to suit their computers, play stations, etc. Factor in the recreation and entertainment activities and make sure you make room for them. Furniture preferences change as do the number of electronic appliances that you need to accommodate. All this requires a modified space.

If you are looking at more open spaces with modern

complexes, move to growth corridors on the suburbs and peripheries of cities. Because they are built to suit contemporary lifestyles and social facilities' benchmarks are raised, you will get more add-ons such as landscaping, cycling and jogging tracks, club houses, swimming pools and other facilities. As they are at a distance from the city centre, they come with cheaper price tags and construction-linked instalment plans.

If you are a professional working in the information technology or manufacturing industry, you may want to consider apartment complexes in growth corridors that cater to these industries. They will accommodate people like you and the facilities that come up will also match your lifestyle. If you have a cosmopolitan lifestyle and like to try out new restaurants, entertainment options and window shop for pleasure, you will do well to look for retail infrastructure in the vicinity. If you have young children, look for premium schools to your liking. Older parents who require medical facilities should be factored in when you seek medical and health-care options near the neighbourhood.

Access to the places that you visit frequently should not be clogged with traffic, or you may end up sacrificing a movie night because it is difficult to reach the cinema hall. It may also constrain your social life as friends are just as wary of endless traffic snarls. To check these out you must visit the neighbourhood and also the unit you intend to purchase before investing.

HOW MUCH APPRECIATION CAN BE EXPECTED BY INVESTING IN BIG CITIES?

Typically there is a 10 per cent escalation in prices annually across city areas. If you are investing in a new property in a virgin corridor where development work is yet to begin, remember that before infrastructure comes into the new corridor prices are very low. As soon as infrastructure work begins, prices rise by about 25 per cent. When the property development reaches mid-way point, there is another 25 per cent escalation in prices. Six months from completion there is another 25 per cent escalation. When possession is handed over, there is yet another 25 per cent increase in rates. This is true for places where greenfield development is taking place.

Take the case of Malini Gupta. She was looking to invest in a property along the Dwarka Expressway in Delhi way back in 2009, when a leading developer launched the first project along this corridor. Since the advertisements claimed that the basic sale price had been dropped to Rs 3000 per sq. ft, it seemed a lot more affordable than the rest of the market which was still holding boomtime values of over Rs 5500 per sq. ft. Malini considered the rates good and invested. There were two things she had not considered—the fact that the property would be ready for occupancy only after a very long time and also that it was not going to be liveable and therefore a dead investment for over five years. When she benchmarked the investment against purchasing a completed property in a less premium area by availing a bank loan and then using the rental income to pay off the loan, she found it more attractive.

On the other hand, for thirty-year-old finance executive Nishant Kapoor, the Sohna or Greater Gurgaon area looked very attractive. Therefore he invested with a premium developer in an 1800 sq. ft apartment at launch at a competitive price of Rs 4500 per sq. ft. The area was early in the development cycle but he had to pay just a small percentage and continue with a construction-linked payment plan. Because the area abuts a well-settled Sohna Road, the chances of becoming liveable is much higher than new-growth corridors very far from established areas. He expects the prices to go up to at least Rs 6500 in the next four years.

There is no rule of the thumb and property markets go through positive and negative cycles. However, normally values do not drop. They simply don't rise for a couple of years as has happened between 2012 and 2014 and, therefore, become more affordable to those whose salaries have consistently gone up indexed to inflation.

Normally when you enter at lower values early in the development cycle or into more affordable properties in the mid-level and affordable housing segments, they record healthy appreciation in capital values in the short term from a low base. High-value properties yield lower rates of appreciation. You spend more to buy a premium property that is in a large format. But remember that since the ticket size is large, you may find it that much more difficult to find a buyer when you are looking at an exit option.

However, the rental return will be substantially higher in a premium property if it is in a corridor that is driven by an economic activity. If you choose not to lease your property, you may end up with a large outflow in terms of maintenance costs.

Anup Nambiar is an avid investor in the property markets. He bought into a property along the Dwarka Expressway, Delhi, when it was pre-launched in 2010 at Rs 1400 per sq. ft. Being unknown, the developer sold at rates well below the existing market rates. But Nambiar invested as the project was backed by a real estate fund which would ensure that the project would not suffer from lack of working capital. When the project received the due approvals, Nambiar rejoiced as the new phases were launched at much higher rates. When the project was finally completed in 2013, Nambiar sold the apartment at Rs 5200 per sq. ft and exited with a cool profit margin. However, his friend, who purchased along with him, did not sell at possession and waited for the project to attain even higher values but the market cycle changed and he was only able to get Rs 4800 per sq. ft for the project.

The best investors are those who see a rising value and sell when they have reached their realistic benchmarks of appreciation. If you monitor your investments regularly, you would be able to assess when to exit. It is a good idea to check out the historical property values in your neighbourhood. Assessing rates and trends over a period of time will allow you to understand how the property values have behaved in the past and predict how they will behave given similar conditions. This process allows you to create basic predictive time series models. While this sounds complicated, basically it is a process of using past trends to figure out how the markets will behave in the future.

RENTAL YIELD

There is another return that has not been factored in, which is the rental yield. Property value attains its true potential when the neighbourhood is fully populated. If you are a long-term investor and want to wait for the property to attain full potential, lease out the property and capitalize on the regular rental returns. The basic annual yield is computed as a ratio of capital to rental values. Normally residential property gives a simple yield of 2-5 per cent. When you are looking to sell, regularly tenanted properties yield better results.

Shalini Nagar is an NRI who purchased a property in Gurgaon as an investment. Since she was not in the country, she found an agent who helped her find tenants for her property for over five years. She has regularly spent money doing up her property and keeping it well-tenanted. Recently, she decided to sell her property as she was investing in a different city for self-use. To her joy and amazement, she was able to command prices above the market value because her property is tenanted and yielding regular rental returns.

AGENTS OF CHANGE

Appreciation largely depends on industrial, commercial and infrastructural development in an area. I have discussed how social infrastructure in Noida led to an appreciation in value in Mayur Vihar Phase I in its vicinity. Similarly, the Ghaziabad property market rode the development works that took place in East Delhi and Noida and evolved as the fastest growing real-estate market in the country. Project-specific price increases can be expected across these markets. One premium project can create new price benchmarks in a locality. This pertains specifically to projects that are being delivered or are nearing completion.

I have seen some concepts transform a real-estate market. In Gurgaon, for example, when DLF launched Phase IV as a hub of high-rise towers of different denominations in a single sector, it created a host of support infrastructure such as schools, retail shopping precincts and restaurant hubs in the vicinity, to cater to the densely populated area. Today, because of meticulous maintenance, this is still a premium area of the city and highly aspirational too.

Across town, rival Unitech came up with two concepts some time later that took the market by storm. Uniworld City near South City was one that was launched at premium prices and still sell like hot cakes. The residual demand was pumped into Sohna Road, which at that time was considered the boondocks but still commanded a price higher than the market value. While the rest of the market was priced at Rs 1100 per sq. ft, Uniworld Garden was launched and sold at Rs 1900 per sq. ft.

Later on, the Singletons in South City 2, which were low-rise apartments in rows that was later remodelled in an even more successful avatar—Nirvana Country—with premium row houses packaged in a compact township with all back-up facilities such as power, water and maintenance, set new benchmarks in residential property. This is what attracted Anil Sameer who visited Nirvana Country just before Unitech announced power back-up to the complex. As he had always stayed in an independent unit, Anil was attracted to the townhouse concept and the neat layout. The promise of all back-up facilities in this low-rise development swayed the decision and he paid at least 50 per cent more than the launch price to buy from the secondary market. Today he feels he made the right decision because his property value is significantly higher than the rest of the market.

Ultimately, purchasing a residential house is all about buying into a dream lifestyle. The developers or developments that can catch a consumer's fancy are always the winners. But it is a little like playing in the stock market. Who is to predict what can catch a consumer's fancy? This is why you see developers constantly innovating on forms and structures to enhance their marketing spiels. Design-led living in Bengaluru, Sky Villas in Pune are all examples of innovations. The ones that click are the winners.

POSSIBLE DRAWBACKS OF INVESTING IN BIG CITIES

Land is extremely expensive in big cities. Therefore, the land component in property prices in big cities is very high. As downtown areas of the city become more expensive, buyers have to move further and further away to the suburbs and peripheries to buy property that fits their budget. Moreover, population in cities is increasing at an alarming rate and demand for housing is directly proportional to the increase in population. This is a reason for properties becoming expensive in big cities.

To get the best returns out of investing in large cities, you should be able to assess future demand, based on planning of economic hubs or corridors. Even as you look at futuristic growth to enter early in the cycle, there are risks involved here. Take the case of the Pharma City in Hyderabad. An innovative concept, it should have come up at least ten years ago. But it is still at the conceptual stage. If you had invested there hoping to benefit from the economic boom, you will probably feel cheated. So what should you do if you see the drivers taking more time than expected? My advice to buyers is to constantly monitor the fate of their property and if there are unnatural delays, it may be better to exit the investment and seek a new location to invest in.

Most development is currently happening along transport corridors emanating out of big cities. They may connect one large city to another as in the Delhi-Mumbai Industrial Corridor (DMIC), Bangalore-Chennai Corridor or the Bangalore-Mysore Corridor. Since transport facility exists and the state of highways has improved significantly over the years, the residential and commercial real-estate projects can hit the ground running.

Transport links can also be used to create corridors of development dedicated to one industry—the OMR and GST in Chennai which was planned as an IT corridor, or the Sriperambadur manufacturing hub. These drove residential development as soon as commercial success was achieved and areas such as Oragadam emerged as premium residential localities despite being far from established city areas.

Buying residential property along these corridors ensures there is steady rental demand from those working here and choosing to live in this vicinity. This helps investors who enter the market in the long term and wish to offset the EMI with steady rental returns.

SHOULD YOU INVEST IN SMALL CITIES?

In small cities, the appreciation is usually less in absolute terms but so is the initial investment compared to the metros. However, with major infrastructural developments, cities like Indore, Coimbatore, Bhubaneshwar, Lucknow and Patna are witnessing growth in prices as well as returns. Always choose a city that has good economic drivers such as IT, ITeS or manufacturing hubs. This ensures continued user interest for re-sale when you want to exit an investment, or for rental returns while you hold the property until it is well-leveraged and gives good returns.

Arvind Jevar is a mariner who has always been interested

in property investment. So when the market was booming, he followed many others in investing in Jaipur with a well-known national developer. He bought on the Ajmer Road where much of the new development was headed. He did not have any means of assessing how his investment would perform. He took basic precautions such as buying a corner plot in a township that would have protected his investment. However, the government changed rules on how close to the highway townships could come up and Jevar and many others like him lost their premium spots. He used his persuasive powers with the developer to transfer his plot to one in the Gurgaon township.

Now take the case of Anil Sawhney whose friend had invested in his home town Gwalior. Anil decided to understand the state of the market and the developer his friend had invested with. A study assured him that the developer was city-based, had a good track record and also delivered on time. Sawhney went ahead and invested in Phase II of the project, paid regularly, took possession and finally sold off at a profit.

So how are the two stories different? While Jevar bought on a hunch in a city he did not know, going only by the developer's reputation nationally, Sawhney did some meticulous local research, including visiting the city and the developer's previous projects. When buying in a new city, check the developer's reputation in the city and try and visit his previous projects. Read local editions of newspapers as they give good on-the-ground information that will impact property values.

When investing in smaller cities, you need to do meticulous local market research. Use information available online on Magicbricks.com to understand the types of property there and how prices have moved over a period of time. You should also participate in online forums where buyers talk to each other about the projects available. There is a strong possibility that the developers in small cities may be local builders with whom you are not familiar. It is best to check the antecedents of the developer and also try and talk to others who have bought from the group. The reputation of the builder and the quality of construction are very important when you want to exit your investment.

Even as you assess the supply in the city, assess the rental demand as well. As soon as your property is ready, if you do not lease it out you will incur additional costs of maintenance, water and electricity charges. Those may lead to a watering down of the benefits of long-term investment. Check if the rental market is managed by professionals or agents. Get familiar with the system while you invest so you can get the best returns the moment the property is ready.

When buying in small cities do not go very far into the periphery unless there are strong economic drivers such as educational institutes or a popular commercial development. Sometimes a sports stadium or a Formula 1 track may sound attractive but remember that that only contributes to seasonal demand. It is a good idea to invest in cities of pilgrim as there is a constant demand for them.

You just have to ensure there is someone locally managing your property investment and returns. Pilgrim demand is steady but needs management. It is relevant only if you are expecting your investment to generate steady income. Else, a caretaker is all you need and it is usually not difficult to find one in smaller cities.

Small towns that are holiday destinations have good investment potential as well. That includes hills, beaches, historic cities, etc. Bureaucrat B.G. Prasad always wanted a house by the sea. When he was posted in Goa, his family enjoyed the lifestyle so much that they bought an apartment in the city. Today, fifteen years later, he is not sure he had made a wise decision. He put the house on rent all the years he was out of the state. However, unlike investments in major metros, the rental returns in smaller cities are meagre.

If you really want to make money out of investment in holiday destinations, you need to be able to attract the short-term visitor who will prefer bed and breakfast or home-stay rather than large hotels. For this, you must ensure you have checked the profile and track record of the developer to attract the best footfall. You should also figure out how you will manage the rental returns as there will be a high turnover of users. It is difficult to manage this while living far away and you need a local broker or friend to manage the property for you.

INFRA BOOST

Infrastructure projects such as metro lines or even high-speed trains connecting major cities can work as good drivers. But assess the future potential before you invest in small cities. Sometimes if these projects are delayed for years, by the time the true value of your project is unlocked it may be too late to register good returns on investment.

This does not mean that smaller-city investments are not viable. If you want to retire to small cities, plan towards it but do not buy too much in advance as the rate of appreciation is more in bigger cities. It may be wise to invest in the periphery of large cities and sell that to buy in the small city that you want to live in later. As in the case of Sobha and Kuttan Nair who sold their apartment in East Delhi and used the proceeds to buy a large house in Trisshur in Kerala and used the remaining amount to buy another house on the outskirts of Kochi. Explains Kuttan, 'While we wanted to stay in Trisshur, the second house which was to give us a rental income had to be in a city with economic drivers. Kochi, with refineries, businesses and commerce, posts good rental demand and we are happy with the investment.'

Is It Good to Invest Near Airports and Railway Stations?

Yes, presence of an airport or railway station nearby brings value appreciation to residential property. For instance, with the new international airport scheduled to come up in Navi Mumbai, Panvel's future seems promising. Therefore, the area is attracting a lot of developers and real-estate investors. Similarly, Bandlaguda, located in South Hyderabad, is witnessing immense interest from buyers and investors, especially for plots. Located close to the airport, Hitec City and Outer Ring Road are the major advantages of this locality. North Bengaluru's property values rose and buyer interest peaked after the new airport was commissioned. Localities such as Thanisandra Road, Hebbal and Hennur Road are all high in investor preferences because they fall on the airport corridor.

However, it is important to buy at the right time. Those who invested in Navi Mumbai's Panvel on the strength of an announcement of a new airport have had to hold their investments for a long time. There was intense speculation and early investors bought at good values. But delay in the infrastructure project has resulted in values having risen with nothing to show on the ground leading to stagnant investments.

Is It Wise to Buy in Educational Hubs?

There are many cities such as Greater Noida, Pune, Satara, Hyderabad and Bengaluru where the growth prospects of residential real estate is promising thanks largely to the volume of users that educational institutions bring to the city and specifically to the locality. Take the case of Shail and Ananth Murthy who invested in a 3BHK unit in Greater Noida. While they originally wanted to lease out to single families, they quickly realized that students were their best bet. Students take houses on lease and stay two to a room or, sometimes, one per room. The consolidated rent that the landlord gets from multiple low-paying tenants can work out to be a tidy sum. However, there are certain ground rules to keep in mind.

Rani Aryan had cracked this code and is happy with students or young working professionals occupying her 3BHK apartment in Noida. She spells out some basic ground rules. First, the lease is made in the name of all the occupants. This ensures that as a landlord she has the verification details of all the occupants. The rent comes in together as a lump sum. There are some shared expenses such as water and electricity, which the tenants split between themselves. If one person leaves the residence for any reason, the tenants put another person in place and the landlord has to alter the agreement accordingly. This normally amounts to Rs 500 as the cost of notarizing the agreement. Rani finds students/professionals much easier to handle in terms of expectation rather than families which are more demanding.

INVESTING IN PERIPHERY AND SUBURBS

Advantages of Investing in Suburbs of Big Cities

There are two types of people who prefer to buy in the suburbs—those looking for spacious luxury or those who look for places that are affordable. Both are possible because suburbs are often less expensive than downtown or city areas. For those moving to the suburbs, spacious luxury, proximity to the metro city, affordable property prices, quality infrastructure and availability of well-managed residential spaces are the key factors. DLF Phase I was a classic example of this. Most of the buyers were those seeking premium luxury close to South Delhi areas such as Vasant Vihar. This is a global trend where people move towards the suburbs because they can avail of larger and more open spaces rather than in crowded downtown areas. Like people live in Pasedena and commute to Los Angeles for work.

Rahul Nair is a highly paid IT professional who has lived in San Jose for most of his working life. So when he was posted to Bengaluru for five years, he was afraid his wife and child would find it difficult to adjust there. Nair opted to live in a luxurious layout in Whitefield which was more or less a self-contained suburb. He drove just thirty minutes to work, his son studied in the vicinity and his wife had enough space to create an art studio while she was on a sabbatical from work for two years. The neighbourhood matched their expectation and they were happy.

In India, the first wave of suburban development was for those who could not afford to buy in the city. Currently large-format living in suburbs seems to be catching on. The best suburbs are those that offer lifestyles and not just housing units. After a point, they become lifestyle destinations for those living in the city and the suburb takes on an aspirational tone as well. Gurgaon in Delhi NCR and Whitefield in Bengaluru are typical examples.

Why Are Suburbs the Preferred Investment Hubs?

As city centres become tediously expensive in commercial real estate, secondary business districts have been evolving close to the suburbs. In Mumbai, Nariman Point gave way to the Bandra Kurla Complex and also the Andheri stretch. Thane is expected to become a commercial business district in a few years. In Delhi, the business district has moved from New Delhi to secondary business districts such as Nehru Place and Bhikaji Cama Place and now to suburban business districts like Gurgaon, Noida and Ghaziabad.

As these suburbs are largely preferred by professionals who come from other cities and like to live near business hubs, they are youthful and happening neighbourhoods with robust social infrastructure. Entertainment centres, schools, hospitals and hotels as well as retail options are all available. They have a mix of commercial and residential areas and play host to theatre productions, rock shows and lifestyle fairs.

Suburbs are chosen because of proximity to the work place, accommodation that is within user budgets and good connectivity, and closeness to schools and hospitals and, therefore, a better lifestyle. There is good potential if the developers keep the real demand in mind. For instance, Noida and Ghaziabad, being suburbs of Delhi, have picked up pace when it comes to being the preferred location for home buyers. This is basically because of availability of affordable homes for the middle- and upper-middle class in these two areas.

When Naseem and Jung Khan wanted their own apartment in the late 1990s, they opted for Shipra City in Ghaziabad as it was the most affordable option. However, since they were both media persons and kept late hours, safety and security of their children back home was paramount. The township offered cameras and centralized security measures, there were parks in the neighbourhood and the children's school was also easily accessible. The Khans then moved abroad and when they returned recently they were amazed to see the amount of development and the rise in property values over the years. They benefited by choosing right at low values and holding on to their property investment until the values rose. It also serviced them while they remained residents and offered rental returns while they were abroad.

Advantages of Investing in Peripheral Areas

Peripheral areas are far from the core city compared to the suburbs. They form the fringes of suburban areas and are chosen by buyers because they are cheaper than city centres and even suburbs.

You can get bigger spaces at affordable prices with modern facilities which are not available in old properties or developments within city limits. Rate of return on investment is more in peripheral areas, depending on the location. Take the case of Raj Nagar Extension in Ghaziabad, for instance. When the Ashiana Group launched a township there, the idea seemed laughable. Nitin Kaushal was a young professional who had a small budget for investment in the early 2000s. He visited the location to consider an investment option but did not really wish to buy there to stay. He did not buy because he felt the area did not have much potential. However, the twenty-two odd developers doggedly started hard-selling the area and today there are a lot of buyers and tenants who find it a good area to live in. Those who bought at throwaway rates then of below Rs 1500 per sq. ft are now benefiting by more than 100 per cent rise in values. Although the investments were small, the returns have been very attractive in percentage terms.

If you are investing in peripheral areas, ensure that you opt for places with more greenery and open spaces. So after the initial stage, when the locality starts filling up, the rate of return will be much better than otherwise.

Disadvantages of Investing in Peripheral Areas

Since Indian town planning does not precede development, peripheral areas suffer from lack of access and security concerns until occupancy rises. Public transport normally comes only after there is a critical mass of residents and this leads to poor public transport and connectivity to city centres for the initial few years. Time and again infrastructure is not even planned for and even if it is in the pipeline, it takes very long to get off the ground. Of late, early settlers in peripheral areas are serviced by basic amenities such as water, electricity, etc. through diesel generators and water tankers. This is where the strength of the developer comes in. There are those such as DLF and Ansals which tried to create their own infrastructure until the population and facilities reached benchmark levels. However, many only focus on the on-site infrastructure and let the residents fend for themselves. This leads to poor quality of life.

Mira Road, off Mumbai, is a classic example where those who could afford small ticket sizes started buying. However, with properties ready and infrastructure not keeping pace, many have started moving to adjoining areas in Navi Mumbai and letting out their homes. As I said before, today consumers are not simply buying a house, they are looking for a lifestyle. So if you are buying in peripheral areas, ensure that infrastructure too is planned well ahead.

Checklist for Peripheral Areas

Infrastructure in the area and connectivity to key commercial and business hubs is the first thing you should look for. Since most developers in new areas are small local players, checking out the builder's reputation and potential to deliver is important. A buyer should also carefully check points like the builder's experience, number of projects completed and delivered, the banking institutions involved and present buying options available to suit their requirements.

Compare prices of similar properties through checklists in newspapers and websites such as Magicbricks.com to see whether you are getting a good deal on your property.

It is better to buy at the beginning of a development cycle in peripheral areas as it will take at least 4-5 years to become liveable. However, buy in peripheral areas only if you have a long-term investment perspective. There may be many factors that can delay the possession such as slow development of urban infrastructure and transport corridors.

Investing Near Highways and Expressways

Today, India is moving towards transit-oriented development where most residential extensions are taking place along transport arteries out of the city. As a result, townships are coming up along expressways and national highways. These highways provide good connectivity to both far-off and nearby places, thus bringing appreciation in prices due to increased demand. However, highways are also not very comfortable to stay close to as there is the noise of constant vehicular movement which also generates a lot of dust. Remember that highways have heavy vehicular traffic and you will always have to drive alongside trucks and buses when driving out of your house.

In metros, highways and expressways open up new avenues or development zones which form part of a larger master plan. You should keep a horizon of four to five years while investing around new expressways. Many investors who bought along the Ajmer Highway, off Jaipur City, had to readjust their expectations after the government laid down norms on the setbacks from highways for township development.

What really opens up new avenues is connectivity. If you look at Delhi-NCR, Gurgaon is one area where new axis corridors are opening—whether it is the Northern

Peripheral Road, the KMP Highway or the Southern Peripheral Road. These bring the area under the development zone. Similarly, Ghaziabad development is taking place along National Highway 24 and 58. Visit the area, consider the pros and cons before you take the plunge. After all, the quality of your life in the future depends on your correct estimates today.

4

CHOOSING THE RIGHT DEVELOPER AND BROKER

WHO IS A DEVELOPER?

Until now we discussed the choice of property and the location to buy it in. There is now a very important segment of the property market that you have to deal with before you become the proud owner of your own property: developers and brokers.

Developers are those entities that aggregate the land, plan projects, secure approvals from development authorities or town and country planning offices, build the property and then sell them to retail buyers like you. Once you decide on a developer, you will be linked to him for the years when the project is under development and construction, until it is finally handed over. In many instances, developers continue to manage the maintenance of the project even after it is handed over to the buyers.

A developer is the agency that conceives the project and then secures permission to build it. Normally marketing is done to retail consumers by the developer. A builder is, globally, the contractor who executes the actual construction. In India, the terms developer and builder are used interchangeably.

CHOOSING A DEVELOPER

There are many kinds of developers in the market. Many consumers have come to me asking how to choose a developer who will deliver the goods. There are large national developers with footprints across cities. Because of the brand value, their projects are likely to come with a premium tag. Then there are strong local developers who choose to remain within a city or part of a city but whose work have earned them distinction. Then there are a host of small local developers who may have been brokers or land bankers but have now entered the real-estate market for the first time and build on individual plots or on small pieces of land. These projects and properties may be much lower priced but you have no means of checking their timely delivery.

It is always advisable to go for a reputed agent and developer, especially for property that is under construction, because it covers a great part of the risk. However, it is imperative to scrutinize the track record of the developer's delivery in the past to assess whether the project will be delivered on time. Also, follow news reports about the developer. If there is some problem going on in one project, it is likely to impact other projects as well.

For instance, when Gunjan Parikh came to India from South East Asia where she and her husband had lived for over a decade, her only consideration was to stay in a cosmopolitan part of Gurgaon city where her husband's office was. She checked out the layout of the city and its profile and finally isolated a well-known developer to invest with. To secure a like-minded neighbourhood, she chose a premium property to buy into. With a developer having market standing, you can be assured of the title and delivery. You may end up paying slightly more than the prevailing market rates, but it is worth the effort and will give you peace of mind.

Mental Notes While Buying Property

- Check for all the legal pre-qualifications and due diligence mentioned earlier.
- Choose a builder who has a good track record.
- Ask how many million square feet he has already constructed and how many projects are underway.
- Check out his past track record for timely delivery.
- If listed, check out balance sheet and quarterly reports to see how the company has been faring financially.
- Check if the project you are interested in is a Joint Venture (JV). If so, check out the JV partner as well and the details of the JV.

- Examine the neighbourhood market, features and rates of other re-sale properties. As soon as you benchmark a property on the corridor, you will be able to decide if the price asked for is justified or not.

Look for a developer with a reputation for quality construction, timely delivery and with an intent to adopt legal practices. Smaller developers tend to cut corners and not adhere to rules. There is a strong probability that they may not be available for recourse if something goes wrong after you buy from them. Ultimately, it is not the size of the development or the developer that matters. Do not be tempted to buy from unknown developers because they are offering rates below prevailing market rates. There is no reason for any developer with good credentials to do so. Check the project details carefully and get them vetted by experts to be sure you have understood why a discount is being offered.

While there are no formal ways of securing this information, there is a move towards structured data in the market now. Magicbricks Advice has been putting together many tools that would help you assess many of the issues mentioned above. However, in the absence of formal sources to check the details, every buyer must do a lot of homework to ensure they have made the correct choice.

A good way to begin is to create your own checklist. What are the five things that you must have in your residential property? For some the locality is of prime importance. Then begin with that in your list. For others, it is the developer's name and reputation. In many instances, saying you stay in a property built by a market leader carries a snob value. For yet another category of buyers, the most important thing is to have a features-packed house that will spell comfort and luxury. These buyers do not mind investing with relatively unknown developers so long as the specifications promised are rich and the best that money can buy. For working couples, proximity to workplaces and safety of the complex, so that young children and old parents can be left behind without worrying about their well-being, is important. For young professionals, entertainment options and safe neighbourhoods where you can return late at night without having to worry about safety is crucial.

Now make your checklist in the order of your preference. This helps you to choose. For instance, if the locality is your starting point, check out the developers who are building there and see which one suits your budget. If budget is your starting point, use that to shortlist developers and localities that suit your requirement. And so on. Finally you will have a list of developers and projects with which you can start your search.

Your Checklist for a Developer

- When did the developer commence operations?
- How many projects has he completed?
- How many cities has he built in?
- How many of his projects are currently live?

- What percentage of price escalation has his projects seen and in what time period?
- How are the values in his projects compared to others in the locality?
- How well does he maintain the development after handing over possession to residents?
- Are there any serious engineering flaws such as seepage or water collection in older projects?

Shaila and Raj Nair were NRIs who had decided to buy a property in Kerala for future use. As they did not reside in India, they had to be doubly careful before buying the property. Fortunately for them, they had friends and family to advise them. However, the first thing the couple did was to make a checklist on what type of property they wanted. Since they would be much older when they returned to India than when they left, they decided to look for apartments rather than standalone houses which were the norm in Kerala. Friends and family suggested names of developers who were reliable and had a good track record. This became the starting point.

Since they were used to a premium lifestyle in their country of residence, they chose to look for an apartment that was over 3000 sq. ft. Being used to luxury amenities, they searched for clubs, concierges, proximity to premium retail options and hospitals and hotels. This narrowed their options to four developments. Now they visited Kerala and personally went to each of the locations. Despite the fact that they were all under construction, conversations with friends and neighbours in the city revealed which projects were developing at a rapid pace.

Now that the projects were shortlisted, they needed to pinpoint the final choice. As they were in various stages of construction, they went with the available unit that best suited their needs. Since they found projects where the developers still had units available with them, they paid the money directly to the developer and secured a bank loan for the rest of the payment.

For Sheila Purnia, a well-placed executive who was posted from Delhi to Hyderabad, the choice was made after she went to the city. As she was working in Hitec City, she decided to stay in the vicinity and go with a premium developer's project. It helped that the city had the lowest values among the IT-driven cities and she chose a well-known developer's project. Today, she has a safe neighbourhood, drives a mere 3km to work, has an enviable lifestyle because most of her senior colleagues live close by, socializes frequently and has good retail and entertainment options in close proximity.

Property buying has to be a combination of many factors and just going for a developer that you have heard good things about does not mean you will be happy in that project. On the other hand, a small local developer on a first project can give you a fantastic property. So go with ground issues and features that will make your life comfortable.

Association Membership

There are currently two major associations that developers in India are aligned to: the Confederation of Real Estate Developers Associations of India (CREDAI) and National Real Estate Development Council (NAREDCO).

CREDAI has been doing a lot of good work in terms of making developers sign the pledge for good ethics and evolving a model code for them to follow. In many cases, as members of these associations, when any developer slips on time schedules or quality, peer pressure is used to make them adhere to the norms.

However, in the event of a developer not being a member of either association and being lax about adhering to the rules, there is no mandatory code that can be enforced. In such cases, consumers have to resort to consumer courts and the legal machinery. This is tedious and individual consumers taking on large organizations often run into trouble. However, of late, consumers have started forming associations of buyers and use group pressure or internet campaigns to get issues resolved. In many cases where the default has been contrary to consumer laws, many developers have been booked and pulled up by consumer courts. This is faster than the general legal processes.

The government has declared its intent to create a climate of transparency in the real-estate sector through consumer-friendly regulatory mechanisms. Whenever that happens, buying from developers without being in constant fear of default may be possible.

Banker's Due Diligence

Despite the fact that every state government has lists of documents required for registration, currently, there is no public portal where all approvals are displayed. However, many consumers use the due diligence done by lenders such as banks and financial institutions that finance your loans as a proxy to making a safe transaction.

REGISTERING YOUR PROPERTY

Registering your property agreement protects you. When Jaya and Vikas Khanna bought an apartment from a developer, they started out by signing an Agreement to Sell. This was the first document that was signed between the developer and the buyer. Their lawyer advised them to register this agreement as it would hold as a provisional document to protect their transaction. While most buyers don't register the agreement to sell, they decided to do this to be sure.

The moment a construction is complete, the developer has to secure a Completion Certificate before handing over possession to buyers. Do ensure this certificate is in place before you take possession of the property. In an unregulated market, many development authorities delay this document and developers hand over possession to buyers before the Completion Certificate is obtained. There are many legal implications to this. Without a Completion Certificate, the project is deemed under development and attracts service taxes.

Only once the property is out of the purview of the development cycle can it be deemed complete and registered in the name of the buyer. This should be done within four months of taking possession of the property as the stamp paper is valid for four months only and will have to be re-drafted if that period lapses. Please note that an agreement with a blank date is really no agreement and therefore cannot be implemented. Also read the agreement carefully. It is a good idea to get a legal expert to go through your property papers as it is impossible for a layperson to understand the nuances of the terms.

Other Charges You May Incur

When you purchase an apartment from a builder, there are a host of transaction charges that you have to incur before the property transaction is complete. This includes registration and stamp duty charges, payments for water and electricity meters, payment for parking slots, external and internal development charges, transfer and mutation charges, service tax, etc. Many of these are payable to the municipal authorities and some are paid to the developer. After you take possession, the other routine charges are maintenance, security, water and power charges, etc. You must read the fine print to plan your budget properly.

Built-up and Carpet Areas

Girish Makan bought a 2200-sq. ft apartment three years ago and was looking forward to staying in a house that was substantially larger than his current apartment of 1200 sq. ft. However, when the construction was complete and he visited the apartment, he was shocked to see that his new apartment was a mere 1400 sq. ft of usable carpet area. Upon enquiry, he realized that he had paid for super area which included lift lobbies, corridors, open areas, etc. and finally had just over 60 per cent of the area that he actually paid for. He figured that he had actually paid per square foot preferred location charges and a host of other dues for the 40 per cent that he did not get to use as his own but was towards common facilities. He had committed the cardinal mistake of not reading the fine print.

The application form for buying a new property from a developer and the buyer's agreement is available at the time of launch in the builder's office, and the clause explaining the super area loading is also a part of this document. If not, you are well within your rights to insist that this is documented clearly when you buy the property. You can also ask the developer to spell out what the components of loading are. This may include lifts and passages, green spaces and club houses, etc. Once you are aware of exactly what you have paid for, remain vigilant even after possession of your property and ensure that these rights are not violated. There have been several instances of developers short-changing buyers after charging them for facilities which were part of the super area but later shaving off a portion of that land for newer facilities. There have been several instances of residents having to fight for their rights as they had already paid for these facilities as part of the super area charges.

For instance, S.K. Jain paid extra for a small park beside his plot in a township in Gurgaon. After he had constructed his house, he discovered that a temple had come up on an adjoining plot and the park was going to be allotted to the temple for its own use. He decided to challenge the developer. As he had paid extra to be located beside the park, he sent a legal notice to the developer pointing out the anomaly. It took him a few months to fight it out but eventually he won because he had documents to prove that the agreement stated that the open area next to his plot would remain a park.

Project Delays

Projects can be delayed for various reasons. Often the development authority delays approvals to the developer. One has to ask the developer to furnish copies of the approvals received from statutory bodies like the municipal authorities, development authorities, etc. This normally impacts a buyer who has bought on pre-launch rates. Take the case of Capt. Anesh Jhala who booked a plot with a premium developer in a project in Jaipur. When the project finally received its approvals, it was well away from the planned layout. Now Jhala's extra payment for a corner plot at a location close to the expressway did not hold and he had to settle for the next best. Because of the abnormal delay in approvals it was not possible for him to reinvest in another project as property values had already risen during that year of waiting.

Most Agreements for Sale/Allotment Letters carry penalties that developers undertake to pay as compensation to buyers for unnatural delays. Check these out when you purchase the unit. In the unstructured market conditions that prevail, there may be other risks. For instance, when Mrinalini Sood bought her property along the Dwarka Expressway from a leading city developer, she chose the developer with care. However, when the development authority delayed civil and development work in the sector, the developer invoked 'force majeure' which effectively meant that circumstances were beyond his control. There is no provision for municipal and development authorities to have to pay compensation to buyers for delayed projects, and Sood waited helplessly for her project to be completed. Good developers compensate buyers with the penalty amount agreed upon during the purchase if delays in handover occur.

Document Check

Manoj Kashyap had decided to purchase a property in Noida in 2010. The project had already been launched and the developer had a fairly good reputation. Kashyap found that the developer was ready to sell him a unit but prevaricated every time he asked to see the documents that showed that the developer was indeed the title holder. Finally, Kashyap dropped the idea and went with another developer. A few months later he heard about a dispute flaring up between the land owner and the developer and the project was stalled. He was thankful he did not pay the developer's down payment of 10 per cent without seeing the title documents.

There is also the case where developers change land use midway during construction and what was promised to residents as open spaces or landscaped areas get utilized for another phase of the project. This was the famous Belaire case where the residents of the project accused the developer of using his status as market leader to arbitrarily change development plans. The Competition Commission of India awarded compensation to the buyers for this alteration. They won the case because the buyers formed a cohesive group and took the developer on as a unified body.

There are some cases where 10 per cent is collected from the potential buyer but the agreement is signed by the developer stating that once this token money is paid, all documents would be provided for verification. If the buyer is not satisfied with the authenticity of the documents or approvals and decides not to purchase the property, the money is refunded without him having to go through the formality of a notice and tedious procedural hurdles. You should agree to such a clause only if your own risks are covered. Ask the developer if the money is refundable under all circumstances.

Ultimately, it is every buyer's responsibility to look after his or her own interests. As far as possible do your due diligence and collect facts about the developer and the development you are buying into. There may be delays in some instances but if the developer's intent is bona fide, then the consumer has nothing to worry about. However, to arrive at this conclusion, the consumer needs to collect facts, check papers and ask questions to protect his investment. There are many developers who follow good trade practices. Go with them as this ensures that buying a property can be a pleasurable activity.

HOW TO CHOOSE AN AGENT

The broker is the third level of professional who acts as the link between the developer and the buyer. Globally this is a very specialized profession, requiring meticulous education and training and also an explicit licence. Brokers are licensed to work in a particular locality or group of localities. Residential, commercial and land brokerages are each handled differently. In India, however, there is no mandatory training or licence and the profession is highly disorganized.

Many developers use brokers or agents to launch projects or even handle continuing sales. Since retail consumers are scattered, developers save on marketing costs by passing on this responsibility to brokers. As a result, brokers know the ground realities about supply and demand. They know when there is more demand than supply in a locality for a particular type of property. They also know when stock outpaces demand and when there is scope for negotiation. For you as end user, one way of finding the right property is to ask agents or brokers working in the city or the neighbourhood. They would be able to give a fair assessment of whether the developer has been keeping all the promises or whether the projects are worth investing in.

Brokers and agents are highly respected, trained individuals globally. So when Sushma Ramachandran was returning to India after years of working in the US, she naturally assumed that going to a broker for advice was the best way to find a property. In conversation with friends and relatives she realized that this was probably not the case in India. Most buyers seemed scared of recommending a broker to her and many gave her lists of those she should not approach. As time was running out, Ramachandran decided to go with the one broker whose name kept coming up as one who had offered good service. She approached him, visited several properties and finally shortlisted one. The broker advised her to register the property soon and assisted her in the process too.

So what did Ramachandran do right where many others had floundered? What she heard about brokers is probably the general statement. But she managed to get a good property at a reasonable price because she went by the experiences of end users who recommended someone who had serviced them well. In India, this third and very important tier of the property market is pretty badly attended to by policy-makers and trainers. As a result, buyers have to be on their guard and choose right.

Brokers and agents are advisers who can take the pain out of the transaction process. Therefore, when Anuj and Geeta Kumar wanted to sell their premium Gurgaon property and buy in Goa where they were planning to retire, they were justifiably concerned about how they would be able to cope with all the formalities. Finding a buyer was not a problem. An NRI friend wanted to buy the property as an all-cheque deal. A broker was needed to facilitate the entire process. They asked a friend who had had a good experience with a broker in the city. The broker not only serviced them but took them through the registration and handing over of keys to the new buyer. He charged them a 0.5 per cent brokerage fee, which he took as a cheque payment, and got a similar amount from the buyer. Today, broker Ajay is highly recommended by Anuj and Geeta to all their friends as someone who can guide you through the maze of regulations during a property transaction.

Choosing the right broker is different for different stages of property. If like Anuj and Geeta, you are planning to purchase a property from the secondary market, the broker sees you through valuation of the property, assessing its fair price and then concluding the legal processes, culminating with the registration and mutation of the property in the name of the new owner.

However, if you are buying a new under-construction property, what should you do: buy from the developer who is building the project, buy through a broker or directly approach an individual? Property is a complicated business and you always need the services of experts. For instance, supposing you were to post your property on a website like Magicbricks.com and find a buyer, you still need a lawyer to create the stamp papers of the relevant denomination, do the paperwork and finally assist you in registration and mutation. A good broker can see you through all this.

Another possibility is where you buy from the secondary market but the property is still under construction. Take the case of Manu and Prissy Kumar who had identified a property along Dwarka Expressway and wanted to get the best deal. A recommended broker helped them with the deal and finally completed the paperwork. Now all they had to do was to wait until possession, when they had to pay the rest of the money.

The bombshell came as they waited—the developer had changed plans and the buyers of this particular tower were to be adjusted into other projects. The Kumars were faced with a crisis. The developer was not giving them the property they had chosen, for which they had already paid Preferred Location Charges (PLC) as a percentage of the cost which was a substantial sum. Even more worrisome was the fact that despite best intentions, they could not find a seller who would take an all-cheque payment. They had withdrawn money and paid in cash to the developer. How was that to be accounted for when the property was shifted to a new location? They pleaded with a broker who stepped in and sorted out matters so that they did not lose out on any of the money paid. Does that sound Utopian and too good to be true? Why do others struggle while all the people mentioned above found good brokers to service them and help out even after the deal was concluded and the brokerage paid?

The problems in the Indian market are manifold. Registration of brokerage services with the authorities is not mandatory yet. This means that there is no formal list from which you can choose a broker. Therefore, you will have to rely on word-of-mouth as the best way to find the best broker or agent to service you. Besides, do what all the buyers above did—ask the broker for his credentials. How long have they been working? How many deals have they concluded? Speak to some of their customers. Check if the agent is a lawyer or a chartered accountant or has previous knowledge of the business. Has he worked for brokerage or consultancy firms or has he worked in industries peripherally connected with the industry—building materials, architectural firms or even investment advisories? If the broker clears these checks, then go with him. The risks are lower.

Do your own research as well. If you have checked out on public sources such as Magicbricks.com, assessed prevailing price ranges for the locality and type of property and also seen what buyers and sellers are looking for, you can't be taken for a ride.

Brinda and Jeevan Kapoor, who owned a piece of land in a retail hub in West Delhi, are a case in point. As they did not like to stay in a primarily commercial area, they bought a smaller and more compact apartment and moved away. The Kapoors had sales offers of over Rs 40 crore from banks, large format retailers and others for their property. However, when they approached the local broker, he offered them a mere Rs 12 crore. They decided to find another broker and found that he too wanted to buy for only Rs 12 crore. Having been a banker, Kapoor soon realized that he was being the victim of a cartel attempt by local brokers who had ganged up to convince him that prices had fallen and that he should sell at undervalued rates. He approached a consultant with a reputed firm and found they were willing to offer him rational rates for the property and there had been no crash in market values.

Ultimately, the onus of protecting yourself as a buyer or a seller is your own. Today you have the means of doing your own research. Check out prevailing values. Understand the brokerage patterns from others who have bought or sold. Ask for references of brokers who have been good to other consumers. These are the best ways to do your reference checks.

As an individual seller, you must hire the services of a good lawyer to conduct a due diligence on title, etc. before you write that cheque. This money spent on due diligence may pinch today and seem unnecessary but in the long run you will realize that this was a wise decision.

Rajeev and Madhu Nayak, for instance, had been seeking a single floor on an independent plot in Janakpuri. Eventually they found one that they both liked. Negotiations were concluded and the money was to change hands on a scheduled day. On the day prior, a lawyer friend decided to give the papers a once-over and found that the developer had clearly violated the norms by building on more than the sanctioned area. On his advice, the Nayaks did not buy the property. A few months later, that property was targeted by the municipal authorities for overbuilding. Property titles and adherence to sanctioned size are important criteria that individuals may overlook while reading the documents. Therefore, go for legal verification.

Finding the right agent is a science in itself. Numerous agents are listed on real-estate portals such as Magicbricks.com. However, property is a hyper-local business. If you want the best services, you need a broker who knows the micro-market well. Therefore, search for brokers who are registered in the micro-market. There are agents who deal only in plots. When looking to buy a plot, go to these brokers. Some specialize in apartments in certain parts of the city. Insert the right keywords and search for the best results. Do not pick one randomly. Make a list of the best brokers who suit your requirements. Now search for people who have been serviced by them. Ask around and you will normally find someone either in your family or circle of friends who have had contact with the broker before.

Consider this scenario: When a developer launches a project, he undertakes huge marketing costs to announce the project so that the maximum numbers of people are made aware about it. The more the developer can create awareness among focused buyers, the better the sales. To reach out to these potential buyers, the developer engages brokers who are offered a commission to bring more buyers to the sale stage. In many instances, brokers pass on a percentage of this amount to the buyer. However, they cannot offer cash discounts immediately. Many offer IOUs which may or may not be honoured and there is no mandatory clause anywhere saying they have to. Therefore, do not be swayed by the small sums promised by the broker. Instead, go with brokers who are known to give good service.

Krish Srivastava, a senior consultant with the UN, was promised a percentage of the amount that the developer would give the broker as commission for the project. This commission would be released by the developer against each unit number and at a certain stage of the project. By the time Srivastava's turn came, the developer had reduced the commission and the broker gave him nothing. The mental agony of chasing a reluctant broker was an unnecessary trauma for him. Finally, Krish went to the developer, found out what was released to the broker, tried to get his percentage for a while and finally wrote it off as a bad debt.

However, there are more important aspects you need to consider when choosing a broker. Besides simplifying your home search, your real-estate agent will help evaluate the proposals that you get and choose the most profitable one. Use caution while you choose.

- Find out as much as possible about the agent before hiring his services. Ask for references. Also, ask family and friends to recommend real estate agents they have worked with.

- Ensure that all agreements between your agent and you have been put on paper.
- Do not pay money upfront to your real-estate agent. This could be a loss to you if you don't buy or sell a property through this agent. The agent's fee is paid after the deal is concluded and registered. You can pay agents by cheque but many ask for the amount in cash.

Brokerage Norms

If you are planning to buy property through a broker, then you have to pay 0.5-2 per cent of the deal value, depending on the size of the deal. In lease transactions, the brokerage value is one month's rental or 8.33 per cent of the deal.

5

MONEY MATTERS

SOME CASE STUDIES

- Sarada Kapoor is a nonagenarian who has a house she had purchased for a mere Rs 30,000 in 1970. Currently, that flat is worth over Rs 2.5 crore. Her four children live in their own properties and make sure she is well looked after. Today she is interested in selling off her property and distributing her wealth among her children and grandchildren. Her investment advisor is checking out her tax liability before he advises her to sell the property.
- Pratap Khetrapal lives with his parents in Lajpat Nagar II in an ancestral property on an 800-sq.-yard plot. He is tired of the long commute to work and

wishes to sell the old property and invest the proceeds in Gurgaon. He has been in a huddle with his tax advisor to get the best deal and lose as little as possible in taxes.

- Roshan Chary is a twenty-seven-year-old banker who is purchasing his first flat. He has heard that a large part of the cost of his property is towards taxation. He wants some rational advice from experts.

Taxation is a critical issue that buyers have to consider when making real-estate investments. It is something you have to think of at the time of purchase, during the tenure of possession and also when you sell.

WHAT SHOULD YOU LOOK OUT FOR DURING A PURCHASE?

If you are buying a new property, you have to pay Service Tax, Value Added Tax (VAT) and Stamp Duty on the total amount of purchase. If you are buying re-sale property, then you do not have to pay any of these taxes. The second property would fetch significant tax benefits, especially when 80 per cent of its cost is funded by loan. There is no limit on the deduction of interest on loan taken for the second property assuming it would not be self-occupied. Considering this, it often makes sense to buy the same in the name of the earning spouse who can enjoy the associated tax benefits fully. However, the non-earning member can be a co-applicant (or even a primary applicant).

Income Tax Exemption

Often, in such cases, the co-applicant who is actually paying the EMI is eligible to claim the entire deduction on interest as well as principal repayments. However, as you may be aware, if the home is self-occupied, the total year interest deduction would be restricted to Rs 2 lakh. I am assuming here that the co-applicant would continue to pay the entire EMI until the loan is fully repaid.

Transaction of Sale

The transaction of sale is considered complete on either possession of house or when the Conveyance Deed is registered.

Capital Gains

The sale of a house will give rise to long-term capital gains. Re-investment of the amount of capital gains in a commercial property will not be eligible for tax exemption. You can re-invest the amount of capital gains either in another house within a period of two years (or three years for construction of a house rather than purchase) or in specified tax saving bonds (NHAI/REC) within a period of six months from the date of sale of the house. There are many conditions attached to claiming tax exemptions that are dependent on a range of factors.

Capital gain is applicable when:

- The property has been in possession of the owner

for a period of more than three years from the date of purchase/possession.

- The sale proceeds are invested in a property which was bought one year before the sale of the property or two years after the sale of the first property.
- The new property is bought after the sale of the first.

Capital Gains Tax can also be saved by investing the sale proceeds in Capital Gain Bonds.

Long-Term Capital Gain and Short-Term Capital Gain

When a property is held by a person for more than three years, it results in a Long-Term Capital Gain (LTCG) on sale of that property, on which Capital Gains Tax can be saved by investing that money in another residential property. When a property is held by a person for less than thirty-six months, it results in a Short-Term Capital Gain (STCG) on which tax cannot be saved. STCG is added to the income of a person and tax is calculated according to the slab rates of income tax regulated by the Indian government.

How Much Tax Needs To Be Paid in Either Case?

In case of LTCG, 20 per cent of capital gain has to be paid as tax if the money is not invested in another residential property or Capital Gain Bonds within the specified time periods, mentioned above.

To assess your Capital Gains Tax, the Sale or Purchase Deed would be the document that will determine the date of purchase or the date of sale. However, when the property is purchased in instalments, the letter of possession will be the date considered for such a purpose. Finally, the exact sale or purchase date will depend on the facts and circumstances of each case.

The consideration amount received can be used to clear loans, but in that case the tax on Long-Term Capital Gain cannot be saved as the proceeds have not been put into another residential property or into specified bonds.

Also, Capital Gains Tax cannot be saved if the sales proceeds are invested in a commercial property, agricultural land or plot. However, tax can be saved if a plot is purchased and a residential building is constructed on it within three years of selling the previous property.

If a person invests only a part of his or her capital gain amount into a residential property, the remaining amount is not exempted from tax unless it is invested in Capital Gain Bonds.

Sell Commercial, Buy Residential

You can buy a residential property from the sales proceeds of a commercial property to save capital gain taxes. You have to invest in one property to save taxes. In case two properties are sold, you can either buy a single or both properties to save taxes.

The last date of depositing the capital gain amount in the Capital Gains Account Scheme is the last day by which one has to file the income tax return. For investing in capital gain bonds the time limit for investment is within six months of sale. The maximum amount that can be invested is Rs 50 lakh. Finally, always sell properties at a price as close to the circle rate as possible.

Land Sale by Non-Resident Indian

The laws are the same for both Indians and Non-Resident Indians (NRI). In fact, the sale proceeds for an NRI from a property in India can be re-invested in a residential property. But such an investment, as per the recent changes, has to be in a property in India.

While purchasing a flat, NRIs are required to deduct income tax (tax deducted at source or TDS) at the rate of 1 per cent for purchase of immovable property if the value of the property is more than Rs 50 lakh. If the purchase price is less than Rs 50 lakh, then there is no requirement of TDS. You need to pay the seller only the balance amount after deduction of taxes. The taxes deducted are to be paid to the income tax department along with a duly filled Challan 26QB. While selling the property, taxes will have to be paid on capital gains (profit). There are certain investments that you can make to minimize the tax you pay. It is very important that you check the tax implications in the country of your residence as well especially in USA, UK, etc.

Taxes will be saved only if the new property is registered in the name of the person who receives the capital gain, which means the owner of the previous property. In case the sold property was jointly owned, the new property should also be jointly in the names of the same two people. One can own an unlimited number of properties.

Deductible Charges

If stamp duty and registration charges are paid by you, the same will be allowed to be deducted from the capital gain amount. Likewise, if you have taken any loan for purchase of the property for which you have not taken any tax deduction under any of the provisions of law, then the interest on such a loan can also be deducted from the capital gain amount. If you have spent any amount to renovate your flat, the same would also constitute a deductible amount. However, normal repairs will not be deductible and only amount spent on improvements to the property will be deductible. Thereafter, the net gain will be added to your income and income tax would be payable thereon, as per the slab system, if it was an STCG.

Pensioners and STCG Tax

You will be called upon to make a payment of income tax on the STCG amount irrespective of whether you are a retired person. Investing in property will not save you any income tax either.

Globally, every citizen buys property many times in his career. However, in India the property markets are still nascent and yet to mature. Those who have invested after doing their homework have made money. As a user, property buying is an emotional decision. For many, bigger, better and more expensive seems to be the criteria of choice. If property is regarded as yet another asset within a portfolio of investments or as a security shield, the decisions can become more rational. As an investor, there is then less emotion involved in buying property for it will be considered a means of wealth creation. Being aware of the rules and taxation details can help you invest correctly and exit when the best post-tax profits can be booked.

EXPERT SECTION

By Sandesh Desai, Chartered Accountant, Realty Gyan

Just as buying real estate is a big decision for investors, so is selling. The profit that one makes in real estate may seem lucrative, but it brings along liabilities in the form of taxes. Since many end up paying a large amount as tax on property selling, a sound knowledge of capital gains and ways to save taxes may help buyers.

The Income Tax Act defines 'Capital Asset' as property of any kind held by an assessee, whether or not connected with a business or profession. This may include various kinds of properties such as real estate, equity shares, bonds, jewellery, paintings, art, etc. The Act excludes some properties from the definition of capital asset and therefore the profit or surplus arising thereof is not taxable as capital gains. These are:

1. Assets held as stock-in-trade for business. Thus, when a builder sells flats, the income is not taxable capital gains but is taxable as business income as the assets are held by him not as investment but as stock.

2. Personal effects or moveable properties such as cars, jewellery, drawings, paintings, sculptures, archaeological collections and any work of art.
3. Agricultural land in India situated beyond several kilometres from the municipality limits.

The income from capital gains arises upon transfer of an asset which is held as an investment or a capital asset.

What Is Transfer of Capital Asset?

Section 2(47) of the Income Tax Act defines 'Transfer' in a most comprehensive manner. The Act brings into its purview all kinds of transfers so as to include sale, exchange, relinquishment of an asset or extinguishment of rights in an asset, etc. Therefore, capital gains would arise on all situations where the asset held has been disposed off in any manner whatsoever.

Capital gains also arise if there is conversion of capital asset into stock-in-trade. This situation happens when a person decides to do business with the investment. For example, after making several investments in shares a person decides to do activities that lead to a regular business. Therefore, any activity which results in disposal of an asset is covered within the meaning of the word 'transfer' and, consequently, capital gains arise. It also covers exchange of assets and would cover a transaction involving re-development of properties where the owners get new properties in exchange for old ones.

How to Determine the Cost of Property?

Cost of asset acquisition would include the price paid to the seller of the property and all such expenses that are incurred to take possession of the property or transfer the property in your name. Therefore, expenses like loan processing fee, brokerage and stamp duty can be added to the cost of the property. Any other expense that can directly be attributed to the purchase of the property would constitute as cost of the property. Cost of renovation and restoration would classify as cost of improvement, and would be taken as cost for the purpose of arriving at capital gains.

What Is Capital Gain?

Capital Gain, as the name suggests, is a surplus or profit that arises from transfer of a capital asset. The capital asset could be shares, bonds, mutual fund investments or real estate property.

Gains arise only when the amount realized on the disposal of an asset exceeds the cost of purchase of the asset. Alternatively, there could be a capital loss if the amount received from the sale of capital asset is less than the purchase price.

As per the Income Tax Act 1961, tax is charged on all income earned by a person in India, but there is also a tax on capital gains.

Different Types of Capital Gains

For real-estate transactions, there are two types of taxes that the seller of a property may be liable for. These are Short-Term Capital Gains (STCG) and Long-Term Capital Gains (LTCG).

The concepts of STCG and LTCG depend on the holding period of the asset. In most instances, STCG arises when the capital asset is held for not more than thirty-six months. However, in the case of shares of listed companies and units of mutual fund, the period is restricted to twelve months. As for real estate, the gains are classified as long-term if the property is held for a period of thirty-six months or more.

The difference between STCG and LTCG is most significant from a tax-planning point of view. LTCG is charged at a concessional rate of tax, i.e., at 20 per cent in most cases and further re-investment benefits are available so that one can reduce the tax liability to zero.

However, the income from STCG is chargeable at the regular rate of tax as per the slab rate of the individual and no investment benefits are available to reduce the tax liability. Furthermore, in case of losses on short-term assets, benefit of set-off is not available against the gains from long-term assets.

Some tax implications one needs to be aware of while selling property are:

1. If possible, plan that the sale takes place in a manner that the asset becomes qualified to be classified as a LTCG, i.e., the holding period is over thirty-six months. When that happens there are several benefits.
    a) Tax on LTCG from selling a residential property can be fully avoided or minimized by investing again in any residential property within one year before the sale or within two years after the date of sale. (Sec 54)
    b) Tax on LTCG from selling any property other than a residential property can be avoided or minimized by investing in any residential property within one year before the sale or two years after the date of sale. (Sec 54F)
    c) If you do not want to invest in a residential house, you have the option of investing in specific bonds of

National Highway Authority of India or Rural Electrification Corporation Limited. (Sec 54EC). However, you can claim this benefit only up to Rs 50 lakh.

2. For the purpose of arriving at capital gains, the value as per stamp duty is taken. In other words, if the agreement is done at a value less than the value as per stamp duty registration, then the value as per stamp duty shall be taken as sales consideration in order to arrive at capital gains. This is to bring uniformity in taxation by both the Central and state governments.
3. Capital Gains indexation benefit is also available for LTCG. This means that instead of the actual cost of purchase, an indexed cost of acquisition is taken into account to arrive at the LTCG. This provision is made to give effect to the inflationary trends and reduce the effect of inflation on the gains. Therefore, what gets taxed is the gain over inflation, and if the gain is less than the inflation, then nothing is taxable as capital gain.
4. As per Section 54/54F, an inhabitable house would not be equated to a residential house. Thus all expenditure made on making the house habitable like flooring, painting, sanitary work, etc., would qualify for deduction while calculating the gains. A debate can arise when huge sums are incurred in interior decoration as to whether this expenditure was strictly necessary to make it habitable.
5. You can claim deduction u/s (under section) 54 in case of investing in not more than one residential house.
6. Purchases in joint names qualify for tax exemptions as per the Income Tax Act.

6

LEGAL ADVICE

LEGAL PERSPECTIVE

Puneet Guru had seen his colleagues profiting by investing in property that was in the pre-launch phase. His friends assured him that although there were risks involved in buying before a formal launch, it was a risk worth taking. Guru, though usually not a risk-taker, decided to take the plunge and bought from a moderately known developer at the pre-launch stage. He was happy when the demand for the next instalment came, because that showed the intent to raise funds and proceed with the project. He had not checked out the property before committing to the developer and paying the first instalment.

On a family trip past that locality, he decided to swing by the project site to show off his purchase. His broker had assured him that the property was indeed doing well and development work was in full swing. He had been told that the agreement to sell would soon be issued. Imagine his dismay when he saw no hoarding at the site, nor any sign of any work being done there. Enquiries revealed that the project site was disputed and under a court stay order. Today, almost seven years later, he has more or less written it off as a bad debt as neither the broker nor the developer has been able to help him out.

The point I am making here is that it is essential to be legally aware before you buy a property to avoid such mishaps.

Before you start looking for a property, there are some documents you need to produce as proof of identity. These can be your Voter ID card, passport, driving licence, ration card and pan card.

When you decide on the property, carefully scrutinize the terms of the Builder Buyer Agreement. Keep a note of all payments made to the developer for the property purchased. It is essential to know in detail the break-up of money paid in the form of carpet area, super area and additional charges. Ideally, you should visit the under-construction project as often as you can to check on the stage of construction.

IS AN OCCUPANCY CERTIFICATE MANDATORY?

Chandrika Mukul purchased a house from a leading developer in Gurgaon nearly six years ago. She lived in a rented apartment and felt that investing early in the project would enable her to have enough money to pay for the house. She was assured that the project would be handed over in four years and mentally she added another year as a buffer period in case of unforeseen setbacks. She invested in 2009 and expected to move in at least by 2014. She was understandably concerned when she was informed by the developer that the project would be handed over in 2016. The developer told her that the authorities have not given all the approvals and until the Completion Certificate was secured, the developer was in no position to hand over possession of the house.

As per the rules, Occupancy Certificate (OC) is mandatory for the developer before handing over possession to the buyer. The OC is issued after audit by the development authority.

So how do you know a project has legal approvals from authorities? The best way is to check whether the project is being funded by banks because they approve projects and start disbursement only after all the approvals are in place. Ensure that the Title Deed of the project is clear. A defective Title Deed will create problems in future. Ensure also that the building has been constructed as per the sanctioned plan and deviations, if any, are within the allowable limits. Also make sure that the developer has clearance certificates from the Electricity, Water and Sewage Boards and other concerned departments.

Commencement Certificate and Occupancy Certificate are two crucial documents that are necessary while buying property. Check the authenticity of the documents with the concerned authorities. Ensure Agreement for Sale and Sale Deed, duly stamped, executed and registered, are in your possession. These should contain fair clauses for both the parties.

Arvind Jhala had registered for a property with a leading developer in Jaipur. Being one of the early buyers he had been able to select the tower, the floor and the unit he wanted. Later, after paying two instalments, when he went to sign his Builder Buyer Agreement, he found that the original plan had been altered and the unit he had chosen was changed. The corner he had selected had a view of the lawn, but now it overlooked the road outside. His floor too had been changed. He was told that the agreement between him and the agent who had brokered the deal was not formal, and now it was too late to accommodate all his requirements as many of the units had already been sold. He had no way of altering things now.

So here are some important items to check before you sign an agreement with a developer:

- Details of the land on which the project is constructed and project approvals.
- Apartment details: floor, unit number and size along with details of PLC, if any.
- Details of area including super area, covered area and carpet area.
- Detailed cost break-up and payment plan of the unit.
- Date of possession, penalty in case of delay.
- Specifications committed.

- Possession related charges.
- Exit option.

It is only when all these details have been documented in the Builder Buyer Agreement that you are safe from a legal point of view. You are also protected against delays on your preferred options and the location.

Now the question is if the delivery default is at the developer's end, can he be made to pay compensation. What is important to note here is that the authorities will take into consideration your agreement with the builder and not the brochure that he floats around. Check your payment terms with construction stages specified. If you have delayed payment or not fulfilled the agreed terms, getting relief from any judicial agency would be very difficult. If you are ready to accept the penalties for your defaults, you can demand specific performances on the part of the builder from the consumer grievances forum.

When Purchasing a Re-sale Property

Check that the property is registered and the construction date is mentioned. Find out whether the property is free from debts and disputes. Check for 'No Objection Certificates' (NOC) from various authorities.

Co-owner and Co-applicant

Malini Govind and her sister had purchased a property in Gurgaon. Malini's sister registered as a co-applicant so that their joint income could be used to secure a better loan from the bank. However, Malini paid off her loan on her own and at the time of possession, her sister, although a co-applicant, decided the house should be in Malini's name and not under their joint names. Firstly, although the term co-applicant and co-owner are often used interchangeably, there is a thin line that distinguishes a co-applicant from a co-owner. All co-applicants of a property need not necessarily be co-owners.

If Malini decides to sell her property before it was registered in her name alone, would she be able to sell without the consent of the co-applicant? No. If there are co-applicants, there has to be consent from all of them before selling a property. If the co-applicant is also the co-owner, then under the Transfer of Property Act every co-owner has a proprietary right on the entire property unless there are specific conditions in the contract regarding the rights of the primary and the co-owner of the property. Hence, in the absence of any specific term, any sale of the property has to be done with the explicit consent of the co-owner.

Purchasing Property from the Secondary Market

It is essential to check the entire chain of the title documents along with all essential service's dues and payments. Once the property is purchased and after paying the registration and stamp duty, the Sale Deed document confirms that you are now the owner of the property as the seller has agreed to sell it to you for a consideration. Checking out the property chain essentially means that you should be able to trace who the previous owners have been. Later on, this check helps to guarantee there is no dispute with them. Every owner would have executed a Sale Deed in favour of the next owner. Only then is your property title deemed clear and free of encumbrances.

Certificate of Title

The Title Deed is the chain of documents through which the vendor acquires the right, title and interest in the property. There are cases where the seller mortgages the property but does not inform the buyer, so you must inspect the original papers before buying a property. For Certificate of Title, you have to hire the services of a legal practitioner who does due diligence.

Registry Documents Misplaced

Vijay Munjal stayed with his parents. Since his father had purchased the property and managed the documents, he had never felt the need to look into the details. When his father died unexpectedly, he took care of all the other documentation but checking out the property documents was never a priority because he was sure his father would have filed them meticulously. Later, when he needed to convert the property from leasehold to freehold, he checked out the file to assess the documents required. To his dismay, he found that the original share certificate issued to his father had been misplaced.

So the question arises: Can one transact or sell a property without the original registry? In case the documents are lost, you first need to do what Vijay did: File a police complaint about the loss. Then you can apply for a Certified Copy from the sub-register's office. In addition, give a public notice in the newspapers.

Like Vijay, many of us stay with parents and have seen them managing property matters. However, it is good to be practical and create back-ups for ageing or bed-ridden parents. A son can sell a property on his father's behalf if the latter is elsewhere or bed-ridden but only if the father appoints him and grants him the Power of Attorney to do so. This is a document that the owner of the property creates granting the Power of Attorney holder the right to transact on his or her behalf. You can always buy or sell a property without appointing a Power of Attorney if you go about it yourself. You just need to check that all the required papers are in order. For this, you can also seek legal advice and guidance from a lawyer.

Understanding Gift Deed

On her eightieth birthday, Sukhmani Devi decided that she would like to gift her apartment to her grandchild who was not yet settled. She had already gifted in cash and kind to all her children and grandchildren at the time of their weddings and now felt that her youngest grandchild could be provided for through her property. She was advised to gift the property to her grandchild. Many of us are gifted property by parents and grandparents. Can a property which has been transferred through a Gift Deed be sold by the person after getting it registered in his/her name?

Note here that an occasion is not required for making a gift of property. The person receiving the gift can sell the property immediately after receiving it as a gift. There is no income tax levied on the gift amount of the property, especially if it is from a blood relative. Generally, the gift made is irrevocable.

When my domestic help wanted to buy a property, she was sure that she would not be able to afford any property that was in an authorized colony and close to her place of work. Therefore, she opted to invest in an unauthorized colony. She asked me whether it was possible for her to make a Gift Deed for a property in an unauthorized colony. The answer was yes because any self-acquired property having a clear Title Deed can be gifted by the owner to anyone as per his/her wish. As long as they have legal evidence of ownership of the property (not ancestral), they have the right to gift it to whosoever they wish to.

WILL: A DOCUMENT DECIDING YOUR SHARE IN OWNERSHIP OF PROPERTY

Brig. Bhushan Agarwal left his property equally divided between his son and daughter after his demise. Would his daughter be eligible for this equal share in her parents' property if he had not left a will? As per the prevalent law, both son and daughter are eligible for equal share in their parent's property. However, if the owner of the property does not leave a will, the inheritors or children will have to mutate the names on the deed before being able to sell the property.

LANDLORD AND TENANT

Legal issues regarding property often arise in situations where the owner, buyer or tenant either does not spell out the terms of agreement or does not adhere to them. Defaults are the biggest bones of contention.

Eleven-month Lease

As soon as the property is in your possession, you would have noticed that most landlords enter into an eleven-month lease agreement for renting out a residential flat. This is preferred by most owners as it gives the tenant the right to occupy the house for the stipulated period only. For the tenancy of a residential property for more than eleven months, it is recommended to consider a registered lease, as it holds more value and cannot be challenged.

Be Safe Than Sorry With Regard To:

1. Delay in construction.
2. Construction not started even after a few years.
3. Demand of money without deliverables.
4. Charging penalties in the form of interest.
5. Charging for covered/open parking space.
6. Developer threatening for cancellation of unit.

7. Wrong unit allotted.
8. Possession letter issued with dictator terms.

Legal options are available for investors in case they are stuck with investments in a real-estate project, residential or commercial, either if their money is stuck in a delayed project or if they are facing issues due to reasons mentioned above. Any recovery or relief from the developer has to start by sending a legal notice to the developer and seeking the relief one is looking at.

A. Legal notice: Need to be sent by a lawyer mentioning the issues faced by you and seeking the relief you are looking at. The legal notice is also considered a backbone of any civil or recovery proceeding—hence, it has to be framed carefully.

B. Consumer Forum: Consumer forums have been created to help consumers in case of cheating or with any issue related to consumers and the company. These have been created at the district, state and national levels.

C. Competition Commission of India: The Competition Commission of India can be approached to file a complaint against any wrong-doing by the developer.

D. Criminal Complaints: This is something no developer likes to get into. A criminal complaint against the directors and the company can be filed under various sections for cheating, fraud, inducement, etc.

Over and above, multiple options are available through

civil law to recover your money and receive specific relief for the property in question.

While there are multiple options available under Indian laws, it is suggested that a proper research on the developer should be undertaken before investing your hard-earned money in any housing project.

God forbid if you do get stuck, it's better to be safe than sorry. So go ahead and consult your lawyer.

7

FINANCE WISE

FINANCING A NEW HOME

Jay and Vijaya Kamra were a couple in their thirties who had two incomes, limited responsibility and loved living the high life. They stayed in a rented accommodation with enough space to entertain friends. They put away a tidy sum each month into savings account and Systematic Investment Plans (SIPs) and were sure their future was taken care of. They were happy and contented until their finance advisor asked them to consider buying a house rather than continue living in rented accommodation.

Their ideal home was way beyond their means and what they could afford was not going to be ready for a few years. They were also not sure if they wanted to sacrifice the advantage of living in a central location in the city, close to their workplace, with entertainment facilities a stone's throw away, in favour of ownership in the suburbs. More than anything else, they were not sure if they were willing to compromise on their lifestyle.

Purchasing a house is a big monetary decision and can impact your lifestyle for many years. The extra disposable surplus in your monthly income now gets channelled into paying an Equated Monthly Instalment (EMI) to be paid over five, ten, fifteen, twenty or, in the case of very young buyers, over thirty years. So should you go for a home at all and, secondly, should you avail of a loan when purchasing your property?

1. Many new home-buyers get caught in the excitement and forget to consider the amount they need to pay to acquire a home. Over-expectation from your income can put you under financial stress. Your EMI should not be more than 30-40 per cent of the take-home income of the family. If the property markets in your city are very expensive and you cannot afford a property that you want to stay in, invest in whatever is affordable even if it is in the periphery of the city if it is from a good developer and fits your budget. Invest at the launch stage so that when you exit, you get some value appreciation. That becomes your seed money. Most banks allow you to exit one loan and take another. So you can sell off the lower-priced property in a peripheral location and use that as seed money to buy another home in a preferred locale.

Otherwise, you will always be behind the market in terms of finance.

2. When a buyer from a middle-income or high-income group has about thirty years or more to retirement, he or she can invest 300 per cent of their total assets by borrowing for their first house. Experts believe that your total monthly instalment should not exceed 30-35 per cent of your gross monthly income. For low-income groups, on the other hand, it should be about 20-25 per cent.

This is a good starting point and you should work towards reducing this number over a period of time. For those who have 10-15 years to retirement, the capacity to earn as well as pay back reduces to some extent. By the age of 40-45, you should bring your investment down to 30 per cent of your total outflow so the going gets easy and you enjoy your sunset years as much as you enjoyed your youth.

There are many reasons why you must go in for a housing loan. For starters, there are tax breaks on property loans. As a result, the effective rate of interest payable is at least 2 per cent lower than the rack rates as you save on income taxes. Tax benefit on repayment of housing loan is available as per Section 80C of the Income Tax Act, within the overall limit of Rs 2 lakh. If the property is let out (or deemed as let out), you would be able to claim deduction on the entire amount of interest (on the loan amount) while computing the income from the property. However, if it is self-occupied, then the interest deduction would be restricted to Rs 2 lakh.

HOME LOAN

The main criteria to keep in mind is that you get your home loan based on your income and track record of repaying previous loans—this is obtained from a Credit Bureau. A Bureau Score is derived by using the details found in the 'Accounts' and 'Enquiries' sections on the Credit Information Report (CIR). As the score is based on the information available in the credit report, it will differ for different bureaus. Furthermore, it is statistically derived based on a proprietary model developed by each bureau.

The CIBIL TransUnion Score ranges from 300 to 900 points and provides the Credit Institution with an indication of the 'probability of default' of the individual based on his/her credit history. The closer the individual's score is to 900, the more favourably will the loan application be viewed by a credit institution. This is a very new concept in the Indian market, but in the past few years the loan-seeking ability of an individual has been closely linked to his or her CIBIL score. This can be obtained from the CIBIL website for a small fee and the agency also advises you on how to improve your score to credit-worthy levels.

If you have defaulted on timely payments in the past, your credit rating may have dropped. The most important factor is making timely payments. You will have to build a good history by making sure that you make timely payments in the future. It will take a few months for you to build a good history and improve your score. Check your own credit report and score before you apply for a new loan.

Home-loan eligibility depends on your ability to pay

(i.e., based on your salary) and not on the age of the building. However, the quantum of loan depends on both your age and your share in the ownership, in addition to your repayment ability.

Your current income and expenses, including other loans you are servicing, are important factors impacting the amount of loan you receive, which is also related to the property value. You can get between 85-90 per cent of the total value of the property as a loan. This depends on the credit scores of the borrower, the apartment or unit for which the loan is being sourced and the reputation of the builder. In some cases, the bank may decide to limit the loan to the 75-80 per cent band.

PERSONAL INSURANCE

When Shaila Nathan went to a bank for a home loan, she was told that the bank would require her to take an insurance as an add-on during the term of the loan. This is a personal insurance that assures the bank or another lender that the loan amount will be repaid even in case of an unforeseen eventuality. This is very different from getting a property insured, which can be done after the buyer gets possession of the property.

It is always better to get the loan insured. For any buyer of property, it is advisable to opt for a long-term insurance policy to safeguard against future problems. There may be scenarios where there can be a loss of income due to various factors or even accidents and death because of which you may not be able to complete the repayment. An insurance policy takes care of this and most banks offer insurance as an add-on when disbursing the loan.

Sheila Mahajan was told by an advisor that she should do a lot of research before taking a loan so that she could get the best rates from the lender. Sheila had always thought that home loan interest rates were fixed by the government and the Reserve Bank. She was naturally puzzled about the difference between interest rates.

Home loan interest rates differ from bank to bank and across other institutions because of the cost of funding. Banks or financial institutions borrow money at lower interest rates from re-lending institutions such as the National Housing Bank to lend to the retail market. In addition, scheduled banks also have a lot of short-term deposits which improve their access to funds. As a result, a scheduled bank gets funds at relatively lower rates of interest than say a housing finance institution which allows it to lend more easily and cheaply. Of course, it also depends on the credit background of the buyer—the better your credit record, the better will be the terms of your loan.

The difference in interest rates also depends on the terms and the tenure of the loan. You can opt for fixed or floating rates of interest. Fixed rates of interest are good when interest rates are low and you want to be locked into that low rate of interest for a longer time. However, when interest rates are high, it is better to go for a floating rate of interest which will ensure that you get the benefits of falling interest rates in the market. If the difference between the floating and fixed rate is not much, then it would be advisable to lock-in the fixed rate of interest to avoid interest hikes for the entire tenure of loan.

PROPERTY MORTGAGE

When a lending institution gives you a loan, the property is mortgaged to it. This means that until the final payment is made, the financial institution is the prima facie owner of the property. The title is transferred to your name when the loan amount is fully paid back.

The property to be mortgaged has to be approved by the technical department of the housing finance company. If the structure you are going to construct is approved, then this loan can be booked under a home loan scheme; otherwise the loan can be sanctioned with the condition to construct the residential home on the plot within three years from the disbursement date. After the three-year period, if the home is not constructed, the loan would be converted to bear a commercial interest rate which would be higher than the home loan rate.

Manoj Kapur decided to buy a property in Gurgaon. Considering that this was a market which has seen frequent delays in possession, he decided to buy into one that was already under construction. Therefore, he was buying a property under construction from a previous owner. Once he zeroed in on the property and the price was decided upon, Manoj found that there was an existing home loan on the property. His banker was where he had his salary account. He was unsure about how to proceed.

Actually, Manoj had nothing to worry about. If he wanted to purchase a property that was mortgaged to another institution, he still had to treat the process of securing a loan as his individual activity. He first had to get his loan approved by a financial institution. As soon as it was approved, his lender would make the payment to the former lender towards this loan and get the former lender's clearance for a new mortgage to be created against the property. The balance money towards the sale agreement would then be given to the seller.

Since the property is mortgaged to the lender of the earlier buyer, that too has to be shifted from the first to the second lender.

EMI BREAK-UP

The Equated Monthly Instalment (EMI) consists of two components: interest and principal. EMI repayments begin only after the full disbursement of the loan. On a partly disbursed loan amount, the borrower can choose to pay only the interest component. Moratorium is the technical term for the period from the date of disbursement of the loan—when the lender actually starts giving funds to the developer towards the individual house—to the date when the borrower is required to start paying the EMI. However, the disbursed amount incurs interest during this period. This interest is called the pre-EMI interest. Sometimes, financial institutions include options to start the EMI payments after part disbursements.

Interest payable during the pre-construction period is available as deduction, equally over five years, starting from the year in which possession of the property is acquired. However, note that for self-occupied property, the total interest deduction in a year cannot exceed Rs 2 lakh.

Generally, there will be no flexibility in the payment of an EMI, although in the case of younger buyers, banks have the option of structuring loans so that the EMI outflow is smaller in the early years but increases progressively. The logic here is that the buyer's earning goes up over the years and he or she would be able to afford larger pay-outs in the future. However, once the EMI amount is decided and the payment terms agreed upon, it is wise to make regular payments. Many lenders offer incentives such as a waiver of the last EMI if the borrower has been paying promptly and regularly.

Praveen Khare had planned the purchase of his house meticulously. His wife and he were both earning well and the EMI amount seemed a cakewalk. The first blow came when Praveen got laid off due to changes in the economic cycle. He was still confident that he would be able to pay regularly as his wife still earned well. The bigger blow came when she was diagnosed with a serious illness rendering her bedridden for nearly six months. Her employer agreed to give her leave without pay until she recovered, but the prospect of defaulting on the home loan was a big source of worry. Praveen decided to take his banker into confidence. He was pleasantly surprised when after verifying the truth of the presented facts, his banker agreed to give them a moratorium period until his wife recovered provided they agreed to pay an enhanced amount as soon as she started working again. Praveen actively looked for a job and was able to start the payments even before the agreed time. In the banker's view it was better to allow the Khares a period of respite rather than have the loan classified as a 'non-performing asset' which would reflect poorly on the bank's portfolio. This was possible only because the couple had maintained a perfect repayment track record and had high CIBIL scores. If EMI payments are delayed because of poor financial management by the borrower, heavy penalties are charged.

Pre-payment

You can pre-pay the loan amount, although some banks will levy a penalty on pre-payment. You should always ask the bank about the pre-payment rules so you do not face this problem at a later date. Today, it is wise to go with a bank that allows periodic part pre-payment of loans. This allows you to keep paying back the principal amount when you get increments or sales incentives or any other lump sum amount. That way the entire loan amount keeps reducing and the amount of interest you pay on the loan amount drops significantly over the years.

What are the documents required by a bank for

approving a home loan? Remember that it varies from bank to bank. As a general rule, banks need:

(a) Details of the property.
(b) Your salary slip.
(c) A copy of two years' income-tax returns.
(d) Bank statements.

Co-applicants

An additional person seeking to obtain a loan with a primary applicant is a co-applicant. One reason a potential borrower might want a co-applicant is to increase his odds of qualifying for a loan or a larger loan. A co-applicant is also desirable if the loan is for the purchase of property that will be owned equally by both borrowers, such as business partners or spouses. If the loan is granted, the applicants will become co-borrowers and each will be equally responsible for its repayment.

Property Title

A Magicbricks customer wrote to us that he purchased a plot in Pune in partnership for building a residential house on it. When he applied for a loan, the bank asked for documentary proof of the prior owner from whom he had bought the land and the society in which the land was. As the previous owner resided outside India, he contacted the government land office for this document but could only trace the file number. A file number is not enough to prove ownership; you need the Survey number. This comes through the Khasra or 7/12 extracts and mutation entry. Since the actual file was missing from the land office record, it created a problem for the buyer. The lending bank should be comfortable that the seller has full and complete ownership of the property before the money is disbursed.

The title of the property is of utmost importance for a lender. You must ensure that the legality of the title and proof of the same is secured from the land office before you buy the land. The previous chain of documents is required by the financier to establish the title of the owners. Now he is trying to get the required document from the earlier owner which will satisfy the bank in terms of legal requirements of the property. The other option is to offer alternative security/assets acceptable to the bank as collateral for this loan, if the bank agrees.

You can be a co-owner but the title should clearly state your ownership status. Banks require the original title documents of the property for providing the home loan. If the land is purchased jointly, both the owners can avail home loans from the same bank by mortgaging the property. However, the bank may have a condition that both parties execute a document indicating that the original property document is released as soon as both the loans are closed. Normally, a bank does not permit friends or relatives who are not blood relatives to take a loan jointly. Furthermore, the income source of the co-applicants should be regular and stable to be considered for loan.

Getting a loan also depends on the report of the local bank surveyor who will inspect the property and give his recommendation. This surveyor evaluates your property on the basis of recently concluded transactions on similar property in the vicinity, the quality of the house and its upkeep.

Domicile

It is possible that you are working in a particular city while procuring home loan for construction of your house in another. It is legally allowed for you to purchase property in another city. Domicile is not a precondition to buying property any more, except in Jammu and Kashmir, where you can't buy even if you are a domicile.

Senior Citizens

A property loan is a long-term loan where the lending institution disburses the money towards the purchase to the seller. The buyer then gets to pay back this money over a period of time which is dependent on their re-payment capacity. This is why banks ask for your salary slip, etc. With age, the buying as well as re-paying capacity goes down. Therefore, banks do not approve loans for senior citizens. In case a senior citizen needs a loan, he or she should consider having a co-applicant who has the capacity to take the responsibility of the loan re-payment. You can also take a loan with another property as collateral. This means that in case you are not able to repay, this property will be seized by the bank to recover the money.

NRI Loan

The basics such as income, financial obligations and re-payment track record remain the same for an NRI loan, although the mechanics may be slightly different. This varies from bank to bank. Some banks may insist on having a resident Power of Attorney in India.

Documents required from NRIs:

- Valid passport copies for all applicants.
- Valid visa copies for all applicants.
- Power of Attorney as per the bank's format, duly signed by all the applicants.
- Copy of current Appointment Letter or Copy of Salary Certificate clearly mentioning the date of joining, current salary earned and designation held in the company.
- Copy of previous appointment letters.
- Last three month's salary slips for fixed salary.
- Last six months' bank statements (NRE account) clearly mentioning salary credits in the account.

REVERSE MORTGAGE

Now that you have bought a house while you are still in your prime, if there is a situation where you do not have the means of regular income in old age, the property can serve as a means of regular income. In a typical mortgage, you borrow money in a lump sum right at the beginning and then pay it back over a period of time using EMIs. Reverse mortgage is a type of mortgage in which a homeowner can borrow money against the value of his home. This can be availed after the age of sixty. Reverse mortgage is the loan given to a senior citizen for their monthly expenditure against their own property. The loan is given until the death of the owner and the amount is recovered by selling the property after his/her death.

The National Housing Bank in India promotes a scheme in which the tenure is fifteen years and the owner of the house and his/her spouse can continue to live in it until their death—which can occur later than the tenure of the reverse mortgage.

The Reserve Bank of India has prepared draft guidelines for reverse mortgage loans. The maximum amount of loan is 60 per cent of the value of the residential property. The maximum period is fifteen years. The borrower can opt for a monthly, quarterly, annual or lump sum loan.

PROPERTY AS AN INVESTMENT

Ritesh Arora is a keen real-estate investor. He has invested and made money in several residential projects. He decided to try his luck with commercial property. He did meticulous research and invested in a project in Greater Noida and got a good rental return for the first two years. When economic cycles changed and business expansion stopped across the country, there was no new take-up of space and Ritesh has since been contending with a vacant commercial asset. The outflows in terms of maintenance and taxes have been a drain on his resources.

Financial institutions do not lend to retail investors to buy commercial property. If you want to invest in commercial property, you will have to self-fund the project or rely on instalments to be paid to the developer. Housing is encouraged under all government and bank policies, which is why financing for residential property has been facilitated.

So the question really is how to value real estate as an investment vis-à-vis other investible assets. Let us look at a couple of other asset classes.

In India, gold is usually invested in as jewellery to which there is an emotional link and therefore not easily liquidated. However, currently some financial institutions have started using gold as an asset against which capital can be raised.

On the other hand, stock markets yield steady returns if the investment is made periodically. It is far more short-term and liquid compared to property. The volume of investment is also much less than in property.

The real-estate market is similar to the stock market, with its peaks and troughs always seeming to make perfect sense in retrospect. Both markets also reflect the economy of the country and offer good investment opportunities. However, the risks must be understood along with the opportunities. Real-estate yields are a function of how long the investment is held, the location and the rental demand in the market. There are investors who purchase several houses and lease them out for steady rental returns. However, the investor needs to constantly monitor the market trends and plan exits when the markets have peaked. Since the asset values are very high, they are difficult to sell during weak market conditions.

Stamp Duty

In general, there is stamp duty to be paid for registration to the state government. This varies from state to state and also on the product range. Stamp duty calculation also varies depending on the full cost, land cost and property cost being separated every time there is a transfer of ownership. It is calculated on the basis of the total value of your property.

8

RETURN ON INVESTMENT (ROI)

WHERE SHOULD YOU INVEST?

When Vasu and Jagadam Nayar bought a property in 1981, they invested their life's savings into it, availed of the Delhi Development Authority's structured monthly payment plan and paid for the remaining amount over ten years. It was largely for self-use or future use by their children. However, with the easing of home loan rates and the rising income levels of people over the past several decades, property investment for profit has become a norm.

Ideally, it is always better to invest when land cost as a percentage to sale price is 15-20 per cent, so that it grows as the overall property values go up. With land cost being very high within cities, hovering between Rs 7000 and Rs 14,000 per sq. m, it is always better to invest in growing corridors depending on whether it is purely an investment or a property into which you would want to eventually move in. Globally, suburban areas are premium locations as they are rich in land and therefore afford large-format units where the house is significantly bigger than in downtown areas. This normally is good for those who wouldn't mind travelling to work but want to stay in large units.

In India, on the other hand, suburban and peripheral areas have been associated with weak connectivity and poorly planned infrastructure such as storm water drainage, water and power back-ups as well as weak public transport. Infrastructural development has to keep pace with the swanky townships being planned in most cities. If water supply, electricity, safety or security, law and order, road infrastructure, etc., are progressive, we can expect appreciation in land value.

Take the case of Anup and Rajni Nayak, who purchased a property in Gurgaon that they wanted to stay in. This row house cost them a pretty penny in 1989 but they invested in it nevertheless, even though they were happy staying in their Delhi house until Gurgaon became more liveable. The investment remained for a good ten years before they finally decided to move in. Now they have been living in the property for over fifteen years and are sure they have made the right decision. Current or future use is a good driver for property investments. However, the trick is to buy well in time when the prices don't pinch and move in when it is convenient. That holding period may seem tedious but is good in terms of return on your investment over a period of time.

CITY, SUBURB OR PERIPHERY?

There are some basic tips to keep in mind when considering which part of the city to buy in. If you are buying into a place that is virgin and early in the development cycle, you may wonder what it will be like once it is occupied. A good way to handle this is to study another similar area which has come up on the same lines.

When Jaya and Vineet Kapoor were looking at moving out of their existing house and purchasing a house for future use, they decided to make it a scientific exercise. They used budget and size benchmark as a starting point. Then they drew up lists of properties available in this category. The developers they did not want to go with were filtered out. They were meticulous about visiting the remaining properties and going through the pros and cons. After visiting over twenty properties, they still did not find one that they would like to stay in. Each one had something missing. Then they stumbled upon one that was a single floor (Ground + 2 floors) and not in a multi-storey apartment complex. The compromise was on the availability of a lift facility for the first and second floors. The layout, the open terrace and the large rooftop, all matched their requirements.

One of the biggest factors was that the property was near the city centre but just off the crowded stretches. The travel was about 3km more but they felt it was a small price to pay for the peaceful surroundings. When the metro station was announced close-by, like all others, they rejoiced at the connectivity. However, now that the facility has come up, the access problems are fixed but the serenity of the environment has taken a beating.

Infrastructure facilities can dramatically alter the living conditions in any micro-market. Therefore, let your decision to buy be based on more macro issues and not whether there will be no traffic or crowds. Urban spaces are dynamic and respond to small changes in liveability.

If the neighbourhood and the property match your requirements, go for it. There will never be one hundred per cent match with your dream house for all times. Remember, your needs change too. However, for the present, be open enough to fit your future with that of your neighbourhood. Normally with the enhanced infrastructure comes enhanced value too. Therefore, for the Kapoors, the peaceful surroundings gave way to a more crowded neighbourhood but the value spiked by several notches.

Identifying a suitable location is one of the most important tasks in buying a property. Users are normally very particular about choosing the best location to reap good returns on their investment. Connectivity to the city and other locations plays a vital role in boosting the re-sale value. The buyer should ensure the property is located in an area with good connectivity to the bus station, railway station, airport and super markets, etc.

All this can be ensured if you do comprehensive research. Get on to the web and start the search process. Now do a physical survey of the projects. Invest in projects that are at least 25-30 per cent complete as these will be comfortable in terms of approvals. Even if you have selected the property, ask around and see what the local brokers are offering as a price benchmark. Brokers may sometime offer better rates than the developer's sales team. You may go back and negotiate with the developer or purchase from the broker himself. But, whatever the discount you negotiate with the broker, it is better to take it upfront. Future discounts tied to transfer of cash from developers to brokers, who will then pay you the discounted amount, are often fraught with risk as explained earlier. Bank approved projects are preferred because they are checked by the bankers for due diligence. Many meticulous buyers avail of independent legal services to get property title verifications done. This is a healthy practice.

What not to do: A friend told me recently that he was working with a budget of over Rs 1.2 crore and wanted to buy a house for future use in the next five years. However, following some kind of herd mentality, or perhaps plain laziness, he was planning to buy within a development in which a colleague had also invested. The logic was that if my colleague is interested—he has done his homework—I would be interested too.

Five Common Mistakes to Avoid:

1. Do not buy into a development because a friend or colleague bought there. Understand where you want to live as an end-user. This includes the location—near your friends and family, close to places you often visit, a neighbourhood in which you would be comfortable, etc. Your relatives or friends may not live where your friend's relatives or friends stay.
2. Do not go for any development or developer by hearsay. Check out the location, the sample flat or even earlier developments by the developer. If there are seepages, weak maintenance or bad parking issues, avoid that development.
3. Do not assume that just because a property is in your budget, it is the right one for you. While affordability is very important, it is also important to make a checklist of features that are important to you, e.g., safety, east or south facing, view, location, distance from entertainment or retail or commercial hubs.
4. Do not buy without enquiring what kind of people are buying there. The profile of your neighbour is something that you have to live with for a long time. Even if you have friends and family close by, your neighbours and their profiles are very important for living comfort.
5. Do not buy without checking basic amenities such as water, power and their back-ups, clubs and swimming pools and sports facilities if you are an outdoors person and car parking facilities to house your

vehicles. These can become major irritants when you start staying in the development.

6. Do not buy into facilities that you don't need. You will end up paying for these in the long-term but may never use them. For instance, if you are not sporty at all, a sports club membership may be of no use to you. If you have bought into a golf links apartments, you don't need a golf course membership unless you are a player. If you take on services that you are unlikely to use, there will be regular payments of maintenance charges and your cost of living will go up unnecessarily.

Terms of Investment

Himani Arya bought a farmland in 2005 upon advice from a friend. In 2007, she listened to the same friend and sold it at a massive profit. However, the second property in which she invested took a much longer time to appreciate and also the rate of growth of her investment value was much lower. She was puzzled as she had tasted quick success and was expecting that to continue. It is impossible to predict a return in a span of 2-3 years. Himani was just plain lucky when she bought in 2005 as the category was just being established as an investment option. Also, 2005-08 was the fastest growth the property market had recorded and as she was in the right place at the right time and was able to book quick profits. Between 2008 and 2010 there was a slump in the property market and she was able to enter the market at a lower rate. However, the rate of growth of property had also reduced significantly and she was not able to replay her previous success.

Property buying as an investment must be looked at in terms of long-term holding capacity. While in the last two years, certain properties in metros have gone up by 20-80 per cent, in some cases that cannot be an indication of what the future holds. An exit after 4-5 years usually yields good returns. Stock market pros use this same logic when they recommend investors to use a systematic investment plan and put in money into funds managed by experts. That concept does not exist in the present market for property. Therefore you need to be more cautious when buying and selling property for investment as a retail buyer. However, if you buy into legal property and hold for at least 4-5 years you are unlikely to lose money. Also, remember to check out market conditions and choose the best time to sell. If the market is depressed, wait out the down cycle before you decide to sell, even if it is longer than the estimated 4-5 years.

Pre-launch

Pre-launch is a great time to invest but is fraught with risk. A house is purchased at this time on the assumption that although the developer has not yet received all his approvals, it is expected that these will come through without any hiccup. The problem arises if the approvals are delayed. If you have an appetite for risk, you can go for pre-launched properties. There is high risk but the returns, even in the short-term, can be very rewarding if the sanctions come through soon. If you have missed the opportunity, a newly launched project by a reputed builder in a good location can also be considered. There is lower risk in this property.

Arvind Kamra had invested in a plot with a leading developer in Bengaluru because he had heard that plot values appreciate more. Although his plot value did appreciate, Arvind held on for a further rise after seven years because he did not need the money at that point of time. When he finally decided to sell, the market cycle had changed and he could not get the price that he could have got a few years ago.

If you enter the market as an investor, you have to remain in the investment mode for best returns. When values have risen sufficiently, try and exit even if you have no immediate need for the money. Re-invest and allow it to grow in another property. So if you have an apartment and feel its value has risen sufficiently, you can sell that and buy a plot in an area that has the potential for rise in property values.

However, there are a few points to consider before switching the format of your investment. The advantage of a plot is that it will appreciate more. But if you buy an apartment, it earns its keep and the rental returns help you pay back the EMI for the house. Also monitor the performance of property in the market and then plan exit strategies accordingly for best returns.

Similarly, a smaller unit is generally easier to sell and is considered good for investment and rental returns. This was the logic that Shagun and Sameer Sharma used when they invested the small amount of money they had into two small properties on the outskirts of the city. Within the city they would have been able to buy only one house, but on the outskirts they could buy two. Buying a 1BHK unit is an investment which gives reasonable returns along with the opportunity of an increase in the capital value of the property especially if it is situated close to a commercial space. Furthermore, a 1BHK property can be rented out easily. In many cases, the developer arranges a tie-up with an agency which maintains the property and also leases out such property to companies. Such an arrangement gives assured returns.

When Harish Khatri made a small investment into a studio apartment in Noida's newly developing sectors, he was actually investing without straining his resources. When the developer announced that he was tying up with a manager of serviced apartments, the Khatris knew they had taken the right decision. They would be spared the hassle of seeking an agent to help with leasing their property and could allow the management company to get them regular rental returns far in excess of that in the informal market.

Panchayat-approved Land

Aryan Verma and his wife have a small amount of money to invest in land. They know that there are parts of Gurgaon and Pune where new areas are being included into the government's master plans. Although their friends have assured them that there is no risk, they are still hesitant. There are two things they should consider: the fact that civic amenities may take longer to be put in place and therefore the investment is for a longer term and also, as the current approval is from the Panchayat, at a later date, when the area is included in the city, they may need to re-visit these approvals.

More importantly, one needs to determine whether the sale is safe enough. If you are buying Panchayat-approved land, get a legal title check by a legal entity. You would also most likely buy from an informal source and managing the plot without encroachments would entail a lot of extra effort. When you decide to build, if the projects are not approved by the municipal government, you may not get a bank loan. There is the very real danger of not having access to civic amenities like roads, sewage, streetlights with Panchayat-approved land when you are ready to build and inhabit your home.

Leveraging Property Value

Ever since Anshu Pradhan decided to buy a house, he has been doing meticulous research into the Indian property market. He has read that developers make huge profit margins. Does he as a small investor have any chance then of making money? A high profit margin by developers is only possible if land has been purchased historically at a very good price. Currently, in competitive markets, buyers get better deals as the developers compete for market shares. So when a developer purchases raw land at a lower value, he also spends on servicing the interest rates of the money he has used to pay for that land, he spends on developing that land for real-estate construction and then on the actual building. At every stage, the developer raises the property prices a little more because he has spent on raising the value of that land.

Therefore, when you enter the development early, you get the best values and are assured that the values will rise as construction progresses. At the time of possession, there is a spurt in values and you may choose to exit the investment at that stage. It is always possible to make money over and above the cost price because the property value grows progressively as it becomes habitable.

If the property is priced very high at the time of purchase because the developer loaded a huge opportunity cost due to an expected future development at the site, the rate of return may drop for you. This happened in places such as Ulwe in Navi Mumbai when the government announced an airport in Panvel and developers sold at higher rates expecting the airport to boost values. The infrastructure was delayed and the investors did not get the best out of their investments. The trick as a small investor is to be able to assess whether the value being quoted by the developer is based on the intrinsic worth of the property or on a speculative growth. As a small retail buyer, always opt for the intrinsic worth.

WHAT TO LOOK OUT FOR AS AN END USER?

Profile of the Locality

If you are buying for self-use, it has to be where you would like to stay in the long term. Property is not a very liquid asset and it is important for you to be able to stay in the house you bought for at least a few years. The profile of other buyers and the neighbourhood, facilities and amenities that come with it, future infrastructure projects in the area, transport connectivity and state of roads are all issues you would want to find out before you buy.

A good way to begin is to assess the size of your budget. Now look for homes within your budget across different localities in the city. Use the search function to surf the various online property portals to figure out which properties are available for the price you have in mind.

Source: Magicbricks.com

Now assess which locality is convenient from a travel time perspective. Sometimes you may find a property that you like but it may be too far from your place of work or the people you want to stay close to. Make a rational choice between affordability, the type of property and the conveniences in the locality. You have a choice between new, first-sale property, second sale of new property or just buying older property.

When you buy a property from the developer at launch, there are certain inaugural discounts you can avail. If you buy from brokers at the time of launch, they also pass on some part of the brokerage to you via a credit note. This amount is paid to you when the developer pays the broker his commission (generally after a few instalments). In north Indian markets, many users have had to pursue brokers in vain for their promised commission because the credit note that is given at the time of purchase has no legal validity. The consumer normally has no recourse to legal or statutory reprieve if the broker does not pay. The best way to address this is to check with the developer if the commission due to your unit has been handed over to the broker and once you are sure it has been given, then ask the broker for your share. However, this has been a much-misused provision and many buyers have faced a lot of trouble over securing this amount.

When you buy a newly constructed property at any stage before possession, you are entering the secondary market as a buyer. These properties are normally sold by the previous buyer who entered the buying cycle at a lower rate and is booking profits and selling to another buyer. When the market cycles are good and the property market buoyant, there may be several sales during the life cycle of the construction of the apartment.

You can search for the current value of the property on various websites by specifying the required configuration. Once you get several options, compare facilities, prices and listings. These may be posted by either individuals or agents. You may choose to use the services of agents or deal directly with individual sellers. If an agent is representing a seller, then the brokerage is paid by the seller.

The value of the property rises as it reaches the possession stage. Each of these factors affects the quality of your stay and also determines the price that you have to pay. If you are buying for future use, you should be able to compute the profile of the neighbourhood into the future. A good way to begin is to create three categories*:

- Physical infrastructure—water, power, sewerage, drainage and roads.
- Social infrastructure—schools, colleges, hospitals, retail facilities, entertainment options and sports facilities.
- Transport infrastructure—expressways, flyovers, public transport, metro, suburban rail links and distances from airport and railway station.

*Check out this link: http://localities.magicbricks.com/

Stage of Construction

A new property can be purchased at three stages—at launch, mid-way through construction and at the possession stage. Old properties can be purchased either in as-is condition, requiring maintenance and repair before use, or as renovated, re-developed and ready-to-use.

If you are currently staying in a rented accommodation, you may want to invest in a property that is ready for possession soon or you will have the burden of rental outflow as well as the EMI on your housing loan. Buying closer to possession entails a higher value than at launch but being an end-user balances the pros and cons.

Track Record of the Developer

You need to check the past track record of the developer. Ensure that he has been giving possession on time and check whether past users are happy with the quality of construction and services. Also check to see who will manage the property in the long term and whether the developer is part of a network such as CREDAI which brings in a little more accountability to his profile.

Price Bracket

Your monthly EMI should not exceed 40 per cent of your monthly pay packet or you will find it difficult to meet the EMIs. (Please refer to the chapter on Pricing).

INVESTORS

This category of buyer purchases property primarily as a means to grow money. Here, too, there are multiple options:

At Launch

You get the best values and even an inaugural discount in many cases. You are investing in a property that is 2-3 years from possession but you get the best rates for this. Going by the trends from 2011 to 2015, the risk is that your project could be delayed and possession could take another couple of years or so. This makes a difference to those who wish to remain invested to the end and exit the project only after possession is taken and property values have correspondingly risen.

There are some investors who purchase by paying a 10 per cent value and then pay a subsequent second and third instalment before selling and encashing the differential. This money can then be invested in another project that has been launched, and so on. This type of investor books short-term profits. This is a high-risk-high-return game and the buyer needs to be very aware of the progress of the project and the market values. Currently, there are no formal sources of monitoring the value of property on a weekly basis. Local brokers are the best source.

Semi-constructed

Buy a semi-constructed property in a locality in which you want to stay. This will shorten the life cycle of twin payments (rental and EMI). You have to pay a slightly higher value than if you pick up at launch but the flip side is that the expected date of possession will have more certainty.

At Possession

Alternatively, you may want to opt for a property that has already reached the possession stage. Here the values are at least 25 per cent higher than while under construction but there is no risk as the property is ready for occupation or fitouts.

REAL ESTATE INVESTMENT TRUSTS (REITS)

This is a new concept in the Indian market and buyers still need to see how it will play out. Essentially, REITs function like the stock market and mutual funds but for the property market. Aggregators who manage the REITs raise funds from small investors to the tune of Rs 1-2 lakh per unit. These aggregated funds are invested by fund managers in real-estate assets for regular returns. Globally commercial and warehousing property which generate upwards of 10 per cent returns are chosen. Institutional real estate and rental housing property also offer good returns globally and are sought after by REITs. The fund managers declare regular returns to investors.

Thus, as a small investor you can benefit from the real-estate market growth without having to manage the physical asset at the end of your investment. You can also invest in real-estate markets with small sums of money and not wait to be able to afford expensive real estate. Systematic investment in REITs work on principles similar to the Systematic Investment Plans (SIPs) in the stock market, where fund managers allow you to invest small amounts regularly into the fund which manages the portfolio for maximum returns.

REITs have recently been allowed in India and the Piramal Group has pioneered the management of some Indian REITs over the past six years with great success. The funds, registered as mutual funds, are invested regularly in the real estate market. Most real-estate funds in India have essentially functioned as funding agencies to developers or projects, and funding individuals have been largely restricted to banks such as HDFC and ICICI. The slowdown since 2008 and the large volume of default on the part of the developer community has dampened the enthusiasm for REITs. There are several policy corrections and fixes that are required to provide a boost to the real-estate funds market. These include easy foreclosure laws, lower and rational stamp duty norms and effective rental policies to provide a level of comfort to investment trusts that purchase and manage rental housing.

WHEN SHOULD YOU SELL YOUR HOUSE?

Your decision to sell your property depends on the following factors:

Property Market in Your City/Locality

The residential property market is location-specific and the prices vary for different areas. How soon do you need the money? Do not sell your property in a hurry if you do not need the money urgently. Getting the best deal may require patience or even spending some money to add value to your house. You also need to consider the rental return from the property as it will be a source of steady income.

Price It Right

The biggest mistake sellers make is in pricing their property too high. The best way to determine the ideal price for your property is to check with brokers in the locality or by listing it on property portals online.

Consider the Taxes

How much you actually profit after you sell the property will depend on how long you held the investment. If you sell your house within three years of buying it, you will lose the tax benefits.

For Mortgaged Property

Selling a house that has an outstanding loan requires a lot of documentation. So try to pay off the loan and then sell the house.

Exiting the Market

Real estate is not a 'get rich quick' investment route. It pays off only when one invests in a property for at least 3-4 years. Even with a long-term investment horizon, one needs to have a clear exit strategy in mind before one buys real estate as an investment.

Neelam and Raj Kundra made small property investments when their daughters were young, knowing that they would require funds when the children grew up. They liquidated their assets to fund the girls' weddings. Having invested over fifteen years ago, they got a good return on their investments. Had they sold earlier and reinvested to book profit, they may have made even more money but as they had bought property for a specific reason, they were well satisfied with the outcome.

These are the classic small investors who remain invested for a certain purpose and are not in the market to keep buying and selling until they achieve best returns.

Like the Kundras, who were aware of the challenges of selling a house and hired the services of a broker, small investors need to understand that selling property is much more difficult than buying one. Unless you know people who are willing to give a good price for your house, a property broker may be your best bet. Brokers usually have a wider reach and are more clued in to the local property market than an individual seller. You can also list your property online.

Property portals allow individual sellers to list one property for free. It is also worth listing as a nominally paid service as the portal offers additional services for a fee.

Selling the property as fast as possible in challenging market conditions is a wrong investment strategy. The only safe and consistently profitable route is long-term investment. This is why it is extremely important to know what will happen a few years down the line to (a) the property market in general (b) the location and property in particular and (c) one's own finances. A savvy real estate investor must know unrealized gains are meaningless and when to take his money off the table.

The property investor must decide on an investment horizon (period between purchase and re-sale). A detailed analysis has to be done on the tax impact of exiting a property investment. Expenses such as legal fees and brokerage expenses need to be factored in. This varies from city to city and state to state. Pre-payment penalties for early loan closure and the impact of stamp duty on the buyer must be considered. Irrespective of the timing, a property investor must always focus on having the highest quality asset base. This means the quality and specifications of the building, the specific location, the depth of the infrastructure and accessibility.

DOCUMENTATION

The main documents required to sell a residential property are:

- The housing society share certificate and the sale/purchase deed of the property.
- A No-Objection Certificate (NOC) from the housing society.

- If the property has been sold and bought multiple times, a copy of the previous deeds may be required to prove the authenticity of the deal.
- Documented consent in case of jointly-owned property may be required.
- Copies of stamp duty and registered house documents will also be needed.
- In case of property being mortgaged, these papers will be held by the bank and you can use a photocopy of the required documents to initiate a deal.
- The sale deed confirms the land is in the name of the seller and he has the right to dispose it off. If the property has changed hands more than once, the buyer may also ask for a copy of the previous deeds in order to confirm the authenticity of the deal and property.

NRI SALES

An NRI can sell residential or commercial property in India. He can sell to:

- A resident of India—the definition of resident in this case will be as per Foreign Exchange Management Act (FEMA).
- An NRI.
- A Person of Indian Origin (PIO).
- An NRI can sell agricultural or plantation land or a farm house only to a person who is a resident and citizen of India.

- An NRI can sell property received as a gift. The sales proceeds of such property should be credited to an NRO account only. From the balance in the NRO account, NRI/PIO may remit up to USD 1 million per financial year, subject to the satisfaction of authorized dealer and payment of applicable taxes.

Acknowledgements

A very special thank you to my mentor, R. Sundar, former CEO, Times Business Solutions Ltd (Magicbricks), who started me on this journey of finding credible solutions to consumer queries. He taught me how to be true to a consumer's requirement.

We acknowledge the sincere efforts of V. Suresh, Vice-Chairman, National Building Code of India; Atulay Nehra, Founder, Atulay Nehra Consulting; and, Subhash Lakhotia, Tax and Investment Consultant, for taking out time from their busy schedules to go through the specialist sections of the book to make sure the content is correct.

We acknowledge the contribution of Asha Nayar Basu, Senior Partner, S. Jalan & Company, Solicitors & Advocates, who has been associated with Magicbricks from the beginning and has given legal insights to our consumers.

We acknowledge all the experts with Magicbricks who have taken the time and effort over the last four years to interact with consumers (online and offline) by answering queries, clearing doubts and imparting knowledge about home buying, which is often the single-largest investment of retail buyers.

- Amit Grover, National Director, DLF Offices Business
- Ananta Singh Raghuvanshi, Director-Sales and Marketing, DLF India Ltd
- Anuj M. Bhandari, Director, BU Bhandari Landmark Ltd
- Anuj Puri, Chairman and Country Head, Jones Lang LaSalle, India
- Asha N. Basu, Managing Partner, S. Jalan & Co. (New Delhi)
- Ashwani Prakash, ED, Paramount Group of Companies
- Bopanna Madayya, Director, Sales & Marketing, Citrus Ventures
- Dhirajlal Rambhia, Chief Advisor on Open House, Discussion forum, Magicbricks.com
- Gaurav Gupta, Director, SG Estates Ltd
- Getamber Anand, Vice-President, CREDAI
- Hafeez Contractor, Founder & Principal Architect, Architect Hafeez Contractor
- Harsh Vardhan Patodia, Vice-President, CREDAI
- Ish Anand, COO, Just Buy Live
- Kaustuv Roy, Senior Managing Director/Head International Desk, Asiapac, Cushman & Wakefield
- Kunal Banerjee, Real Estate Marketing Specialist
- Manish Sinha, CEO, Equifax
- Manoj Gaur, President, CREDAI, Western UP
- Mohit Arora, Managing Director, Supertech Ltd
- Niranjan Hiranandani, MD, Hiranandani Group of Companies

- Paras Gundecha, President, MCHI-CREDAI (Mumbai)
- Partho Mukherjee, Principal Advisor on Open House, Discussion forum, Magicbricks.com
- R. Murugesan, CEO, ARAM Realty
- Ramesh Bhojwani, Mumbai-based Financial Expert
- Ravindra Pai, MD, Century Real Estate Holding Pvt. Ltd
- Rohtas Goel, CMD, Omaxe Ltd
- S. Padmanabhan, VP, Maangalya Developers
- S. Ramakrishnan, CEO, MARG ProperTies
- Sanjay Chawla, Director, Proficent Infratech Pvt. Ltd
- Satish Magar, Vice-President, CREDAI
- Shishir Gupta, Expert on Open House, Discussion forum, Magicbricks.com
- Subhash Lakhotia, Tax & Investment Consultant
- Sudhir Vohra, Architect & Urban Planner, Sudhir Vohra Consultants
- Sunil Mantri, CMD, Sunil Mantri Realty
- Sushant Muttreja, Managing Director at Cosmic Structures Ltd
- T. Chitty Babu, President, CREDAI, Chennai
- Vikas Vasal, Executive Director, KPMG India